MARTIN PULLEN is a BAF... director of many children'... *Paddington Bear, The Womb...* ...*...an Pa*. He is the author and illustrator of *The Completely Useless Guide to Christmas*.

Also by Martin Pullen

THE COMPLETELY USELESS GUIDE TO CHRISTMAS

THE COMPLETELY USELESS GUIDE TO LONDON

MARTIN PULLEN

JOHN BLAKE

Published by John Blake Publishing Ltd
3 Bramber Court, 2 Bramber Road,
London W14 9PB, England

www.johnblakepublishing.co.uk

www.facebook.com/Johnblakepub facebook
twitter.com/johnblakepub twitter

First published in paperback in 2014

ISBN: 978 1 78219 771 3

British Library Cataloguing-in-Publication Data:

A catalogue record for this book is available from the British Library.

Design by www.envydesign.co.uk

Printed in Great Britain by CPI Group (UK) Ltd, Croydon CR0 4YY

3 5 7 9 10 8 6 4 2

Papers used by John Blake Publishing are natural, recyclable products
made from wood grown in sustainable forests. The manufacturing processes
conform to the environmental regulations of the country of origin.

Every attempt has been made to contact the relevant copyright-holders,
but some were unobtainable. We would be grateful if the appropriate
people could contact us.

FOR LESLEY
The building between the London Eye
and the Thames

SECTION 1 – LONDON LANDMARKS

SECTION 2 – CULTURE VULTURE

SECTION 3 – A NIGHT ON THE TOWN

SECTION 4 – GOING UNDERGROUND

SECTION 5 – LEAFY LONDON

SECTION 6 – A MATTER OF LIFE AND DEATH

SECTION 7 – AND FINALLY...

Section 1

LONDON LANDMARKS

Chapter 1

LONDON SIGHTS

In 1752, the original Liberty Bell was cast in the Whitechapel Bell Foundry, on the corner of Whitechapel Road and Plumbers Row. Unfortunately (and the finger of blame still points both ways across the Atlantic), on its first ring the bell cracked. After local attempts to melt down the bell and recast with a greater copper content to make it less brittle proved unsuccessful, a replacement bell was ordered from the Whitechapel Bell Foundry. The original can be found, to this day, still on display in the US city of Philadelphia.

In 1858, the Whitechapel Bell Foundry cast its biggest bell, Big Ben…

Big Ben
Every tourist who visits London photographs Big Ben; at least they think they do. Few have, as what they are actually photographing is the Elizabeth Tower (formerly the clock tower of the Palace of Westminster). Big Ben is the nickname of the Great Hour Bell housed inside the tower.

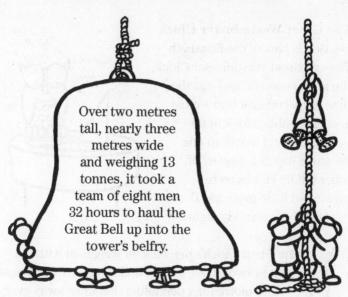

Over two metres tall, nearly three metres wide and weighing 13 tonnes, it took a team of eight men 32 hours to haul the Great Bell up into the tower's belfry.

Unfortunately, not liking the bell's pitch, Edmund Denison, the man responsible for the clock tower's chimes, more than doubled the size of its hammer, until – in September 1859, a mere two months after it had first rung out – the new bell cracked.

For three years the Great Hour Bell remained silent. Meanwhile, a piece of metal was chipped out to inspect the depth of the damage and a hole drilled to stop the crack developing further. The bell was turned so that the crack was away from the hammer, and the hammer reduced back to its correct size.

And there Big Ben has remained until this day, slightly cracked, a piece missing and sounding a little out of tune; a familiar bong that has rung out across London over eight million times.

The Great Westminster Clock

Big Ben is part of the Elizabeth Tower's Great Westminster Clock, the most powerful and – at the time of its construction – most accurate public clock in the world, keeping to within one second a day at a time when other public clocks were proving of little more use than a sundial on a cloudy night.

The Great Clock's mechanism weighs in within a cog or two of five tonnes and sits above an almost four-metre-long pendulum that ticks away every two seconds. The pendulum is fine-tuned by the placing of a small stack of old pre-decimal coins on top; adding or removing a penny will change the clock's speed by just under half a second a day.

Elizabeth Tower

Built on sand and soft soil on the north bank of the River Thames, the tip of the Elizabeth Tower leans nearly half a metre to the northwest, 0.26 degrees from the vertical. The tilt is increasing by an average of 0.65mm a year.

Sir Winston Churchill's Statue

The bronze statue of Sir Winston Churchill in Parliament Square has a mild electric current running through it to both prevent a layer of snow forming and to deter pigeons from perching on the former prime minister's bald head.

Horse Guards

Formerly the headquarters of – among a number of other senior British Army regiments – the Household Cavalry (hence the name), the Horse Guards building stands between Whitehall and Horse Guards Parade. Only the monarch is allowed to drive through Horse Guards' central arch...

...unless, that is, one is in possession of a special pass. Oval in shape and made of plastic, the passes were, until recent times, carved from ivory.

If not in possession of a special pass – plastic or otherwise – then sneak through a side arch on foot, turn and look up, and you will notice that the numbers on the clock above Horse Guards, viewed from Horse Guards Parade, are a pale green, which blends in with the warm grey Portland stone of the building. Except for, that is, the number 2, which is coloured black. On 30 January 1649, King Charles I was executed directly opposite the Whitehall entrance to Horse Guards, on a scaffold erected outside Banqueting House: the black number 2 is a reminder that the King was executed at precisely 2 p.m.

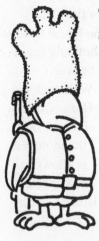

The dismounted Household Cavalry guard who stands close to the stables' entrance of Horse Guards is known as the 'chick sentry'.

Legend tells that a guard was once found asleep on duty. Upon questioning by his somewhat irate commanding officer, the guard explained that (not that it in any way explains why he was asleep) he thought his job was to keep an eye out for the Quartermaster Sergeant's chickens.

Admiralty Arch

As you head into Trafalgar Square from The Mall, walk through the small arch on the left of the central arch of the grand archway known as Admiralty Arch. Protruding from one of the square pillars on your right, just above the passing traffic, is a casting of a nose. The nose is said to be that of Napoleon.

Set at a height best suited to a soldier on horseback, rubbing Napoleon's nose is thought to bring good luck.

Eleanor Cross

Methinks the common-council shou'd
Of it have taken pity,
'Cause good old cross, it always stood
So firmly in the city.
Since crosses you so much distain,
Faith if I were you,
For fear the king should rule again
I'd pull down Tyburn too.

From the popular Royalist ballad
'The Downfall of Charing Cross' by Charles Mackay

In the winter of 1290, King Edward I was visiting the city of Lincoln, when his wife, Queen Eleanor, was struck down with a fever. Taken to the manor house of Richard de Weston in the Nottinghamshire village of Harby, she died soon afterwards. Grief stricken, the King decreed that each stopping point of the Queen's funeral procession en route to her state burial at Westminster Abbey should be marked by a memorial cross. The final stop was in the hamlet of Charing – what we now know, thanks to Queen Eleanor, as Charing Cross – and it was here, to the south of what was to later become Trafalgar Square, that the last of the 12 Eleanor Crosses was erected.

And so it stood until 1647 when, with England in the grip of civil war, Parliament, loyal to Oliver Cromwell, ordered its removal.

Following the death of Cromwell and the restoration of the monarchy with the coming to the throne of King Charles II in 1660, the equestrian statue of his late father, Charles I, was erected on the spot, barely a short gallop from the location of his execution in 1649 (see Horse Guards, page 5).

The statue remains in place to this day, and it is from here – the statue of King Charles I to the south of Trafalgar Square – that road distances from London are measured.

There is, of course, an Eleanor Cross on the forecourt of Charing Cross station, a short pigeon's hop to the north-east of the square, but this ornate copy was erected in 1864, upon the opening of the station.

London Eye
The London Eye revolves at a pedestrian 0.6 miles (1km) per hour. If it ever were to break loose from its moorings it would take 4 years and 324 days to roll completely round the Earth.

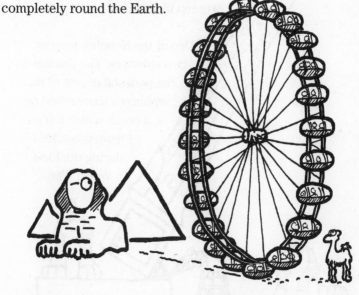

Cleopatra's Needle

On the north bank of the River Thames near Embankment station stands Cleopatra's Needle. Dating from around 1450BC, the 18-metre-high Egyptian obelisk was given to the British in 1819 as a gift by the Egyptian ruler, Muhammad Ali. Not that the British wanted to appear ungrateful, but they refused to pay for it to be transported until 1877, the obelisk eventually being erected on the Embankment in 1878.

Among many other things concealed in a time capsule at its base are a Bradshaw *Railway Guide*, a hydraulic jack and photographs of what were, at the time, considered to be the 12 best-looking women in England.

Also at the Needle's base sit two sphinxes. The damage to the pedestal of one of the sphinxes was caused by a bomb which fell on 4 September 1917, during the First World War.

OXO Tower

A grand art deco building crowned by
the world's biggest game of noughts
and crosses, it is unbelievable that
– in what could be best described
as an urban degeneration scheme –
plans were submitted in the 1970s to
demolish the OXO Tower.

Marble Arch

Constructed in 1828 as a monumental entrance to
Buckingham Palace, the story goes that Marble Arch was
too narrow for the royal state coach to pass through. Her
Majesty, Queen Victoria, was not best pleased and, in 1851,
the arch was moved to the junction of Oxford Street and
Park Lane. Although it makes for a good tale, the truth is
much simpler – the arch was surplus to requirements when
Buckingham Palace was enlarged.

Despite the move,
still to this day only
the Royal Horse
Artillery, the
King's Troop
and senior royal
family members
are permitted to
pass through its
central
arch.

Under proposals to make it more accessible, Marble Arch may once again be on the move, away from its current position on a large traffic island and across the road into Hyde Park.

The Monument

Originally a visible part of the London skyline but now tucked away behind buildings just north of London Bridge, at nearly 62 metres, The Monument is the world's tallest free-standing stone column.

Constructed in commemoration of the Great Fire of London, The Monument's base stands the exact same distance as its height from the baker's shop in Pudding Lane where, in 1666, the Great Fire started.

Designed by Sir Christopher Wren and Robert Hooke, the Portland-stone column, topped by a copper urn surrounded by gilt flames, took six years to build, with construction completed in 1677.

Wren and Hooke designed The Monument with the added intention of conducting a number of astronomical and scientific experiments. With this in mind, the 311 interior steps leading to the viewing platform were all built to exactly six inches in height, so that the column could be used for experiments on air pressure.

Surrounding an open vertical shaft, the steps continue past the viewing platform, leading up a ladder through the copper urn to a hinged trapdoor at the very top. Thanks to the open shaft to the sky, exact measurements of the movements of a star could be made using a zenith telescope pointing upward from the cellar laboratory below the column's base.

Walkie-Talkie Tower

In September 2013, the still-under-construction City of London skyscraper at 20 Fenchurch Street – at first christened the 'Walkie-Talkie' due to its resemblance to a giant, hand-held, not-so-portable two-way radio transceiver – gained the nickname 'Walkie-Scorchie'. The newly installed windowpanes on the concave side wall acted like a giant magnifying glass, concentrating beams of autumn sunlight down onto Eastcheap and melting parts of a Jaguar car parked nearby.

Less-forgiving sections of the media have dubbed the 37-storey tower 'the City's solar death ray'.

The O2

Resembling a single cup of a huge padded bra, it's somewhat apt that The O2 sits on the perfectly breast-shaped Greenwich Peninsula. Originally the Millennium Dome, built to house an exhibition commemorating the new millennium, The O2 is now one of the most popular music venues in London. Actor Pierce Brosnan famously slid down the outside of The O2 in the film *The World Is Not Enough*. Had it been a

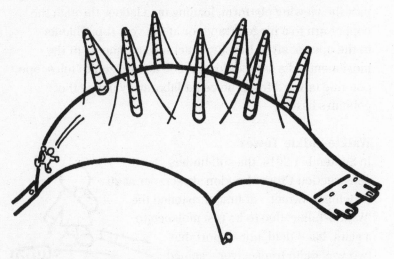

windy day he may well have made it across the Thames to Canary Wharf.

Battersea Power Station

Designed by Sir Giles Gilbert Scott – famous for Bankside
Power Station (now the Tate Modern), Liverpool Cathedral
and the classic K6 red telephone
box – Battersea Power Station is
thought to be the largest brick
building in Europe. Wandsworth
Council estimate the brick
count as 61 million: placed
end to end, almost
enough to stretch
around the
entire coast of
mainland Britain.

Inside, the iconic power station once boasted grand
art deco features in the control room, Italian marble in the
turbine hall and parquet flooring throughout. However, Old
King Coal was a dirty old soul and, at full capacity, Battersea
Power Station consumed more than 2,000 tonnes of coal
and 600 Olympic-sized swimming pools of water a day, in
exchange belching out countless tonnes of carbon dioxide
and sulphur.

Built in two stages, Power Station A was completed in
1935. With only two chimneys, during the Second World
War aircrews nicknamed the station 'Woodbines', as it was
thought that the building resembled two cigarettes being
offered from a giant pack of Woodbine cigarettes. It wasn't
until 1955, with the addition of Station B, that the power
station gained two extra chimneys and then resembled
London's biggest upside-down table.

Generating its last megawatt of electricity in 1983, the following year a competition to redesign the site was won by Alton Towers Limited, with a proposal for an indoor theme park. Work was begun in 1986. By the time the money ran out in 1989 the roof had been removed and the interior left to suffer from the elements.

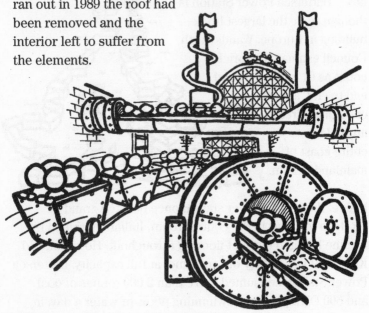

Further development plans in the 1990s included a restaurant with a single table at the top of one of the 113-metre tall chimneys.

In 2006, Battersea Power Station and the surrounding site were purchased by Real Estate Opportunities for £400 million. REO's grand development plans – including shrouding most of the buildings under a thick plastic noise-reducing and zero-carbon temperature-regulating EcoDome – popped like squeezed bubble wrap when, in 2011, their debts were called in by creditors.

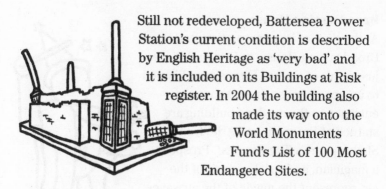

Still not redeveloped, Battersea Power Station's current condition is described by English Heritage as 'very bad' and it is included on its Buildings at Risk register. In 2004 the building also made its way onto the World Monuments Fund's List of 100 Most Endangered Sites.

Latest development proposals include a new stadium for Chelsea Football Club. Like one of Ian Hutchinson's famed long throw-ins for the club in the 1970s, Battersea Power Station's future is, at the time of writing, up in the air.

Tate Modern

With a 99-metre chimney and a turbine hall and boiler house made of considerably more bricks than a modern art installation, what was Bankside Power Station closed in 1991 and reopened in 2000 as the Tate Modern. The world's most popular modern-art gallery, the Tate Modern is a building in which to wander round and soak up the atmosphere, drink coffee and people-watch, or sit on the balcony and look across the Thames to St Paul's Cathedral and the City.

And, if you have time, you can also look at some art.

Broadcasting House

At the time of its construction in 1932, Broadcasting House, in Portland Place, just north of Oxford Circus, was likened to an ocean cruise liner. Above the entrance to the art deco building are statues of Prospero and Ariel from Shakespeare's *The Tempest*. Prospero, a magician, and Ariel, a spirit of the air, represent the magic of the airwaves, signifying that Broadcasting House was built as headquarters for the BBC, and is now home to BBC Radio.

Set in the heart of Broadcasting House, the BBC Radio Theatre played host to the live recording of such radio classics as *The Goon Show* and *Hancock's Half Hour*.

Used during the Second World War as an air-raid shelter, rumours abound that a secret platform exists linking the BBC building to the Bakerloo Underground line that runs directly beneath the theatre.

The BBC conducts monthly guided tours of Broadcasting House, but don't expect to be shown the infamous Room 101 – the personnel office that may have been George Orwell's inspiration for the Ministry of Love torture chamber in the book *Nineteen Eighty-Four*. The room was demolished as part of refurbishment work.

City Hall

Described as a giant car headlight, the Norman Foster-designed City Hall is the headquarters of the Mayor of London and the London Assembly. Once affectionately known as 'Ken's testicle' after Mayor Ken Livingstone, when Mayor Boris Johnson took over the reins it was rechristened 'Boris's b*****k'.

Crystal Palace

The south London suburb of Sydenham Hill was renamed Crystal Palace after the Crystal Palace – a greenhouse the size of 10 football pitches – was dismantled and moved from Hyde Park following the Great Exhibition of 1851.

With exhibits including the 'Koh-i-noor', at the time the biggest diamond in the world – and the 'Tempest Prognosticator', a barometer that used leeches – the Great Exhibition packed in the crowds.

Luckily, the giant greenhouse also laid claim to Britain's first public toilet, albeit gents only. During the exhibition, 827,280 male visitors paid one penny each to use the 'Reading Rooms', giving rise to the expression 'to spend a penny'. Women, it appears, unable to spend a penny, had to pee in the plant pots.

With its fortunes in decline, during the First World War the Crystal Palace was given over to the Royal Navy as a training establishment, gaining the nickname 'HMS Crystal Palace'. Post-war, the Palace fell into further decline, eventually burning down on the night of 30 November 1936.

But, like a glass phoenix from the flames, the Crystal Palace may rise again as, in 2013, plans were revealed to build a replica on the original foundations.

With any luck, this time the plans will include a few 'Ladies'…

Chapter 2

A BRIDGE TOO FAR

Speaking of ladies...

Replacing an earlier bridge that was declared unsafe, Waterloo Bridge is affectionately known as the Ladies' Bridge because it was mostly built by women, while men were abroad fighting during the Second World War. Although not completed until 1945, it was the only bridge across the River Thames in London to suffer damage from German bombers.

Grove Road Railway Bridge

Not built across the Thames but also suffering damage, on 13 June 1944 the first flying bomb to fall on London hit the railway bridge in Grove Road, Bow.

21

Millennium Bridge

Creating a walkway from the Tate Modern on the south bank of the River Thames to St Paul's Cathedral, on the day of opening the London Millennium Footbridge was affectionately rechristened the 'Wobbly Bridge', after 90,000 people attempted to cross it and discovered it was less stable than a tent pitched on the north face of the Eiger.

While undergoing reconstructive work to cure its swaying motion, in accordance with an ancient by-law, bales of straw were hung underneath to warn passing ships of the lowered headroom.

Putney Bridge

After being jilted by her lover, in 1795 celebrated writer Mary Wollstonecraft attempted to commit suicide by jumping from the original Putney Bridge. Surviving the fall, she met and married famed philosopher William Godwin and gave birth to two daughters. Elder daughter, Mary, went on to marry poet Percy Shelley and write the novel *Frankenstein*.

Tower Bridge

With its imposing towers and gothic spires, despite being the iconic image of picture-postcard London, Tower Bridge is one of the most modern of London bridges. Built in 1894, when tall ships still sailed up the Thames to deliver their goods to the Port of London, the bridge was designed with pivoting bascules – counterbalanced levers – which rose to let river traffic through.

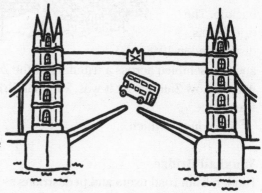

In 1952, a number 78 bus was crossing the bridge when safety procedures failed and the southern bascule started to rise. Unable to stop in time, quick-thinking driver Albert Gunter accelerated – and successfully shot across the one-metre gap.

Richmond Lock Footbridge

One wonders just how effective the sluice gates of Richmond Lock Footbridge are, as Richmond is often liable to flooding. This is in evidence at the nearby White Cross pub, where a sign with an arrow pointing to the second floor declares: ENTRANCE AT HIGH TIDE.

Opened in 1894, Richmond Lock Footbridge is one of the most striking bridges across the River Thames.

Millbank Bridge

With worries that Luftwaffe bombs might put Vauxhall Bridge out of use during the Second World War, Millbank Bridge was built alongside as a backup. The bridge was dismantled in 1948

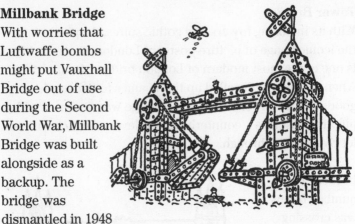

and reassembled across a tributary of the Zambezi river, in what is now Zambia. As it was, Vauxhall Bridge survived the war intact.

Speaking of which…

Vauxhall Bridge

Hidden from road users and pedestrians as they pass above, both sides of Vauxhall Bridge are decorated with four female bronze statues. One of the statues is holding a miniature of St Paul's Cathedral. Known as 'Little St Paul's on the Water', this is the smallest cathedral in London.

In 1966, the opening sequence of the Michael Caine film *Alfie* was filmed on Vauxhall Bridge.

Not a lot of people…

Chapter 3

GET ME TO THE CHURCH ON TIME

Stand outside St Peter upon Cornhill church, at the eastern end of Cornhill in the City of London; look up, and you will see three angry devils staring down at you from the office block to the left. The story goes that the original plans for the building of the office block stole a foot of the church's land. Forced to redraw his plans, the architect took revenge by placing the gargoyle devils on the roof to curse anyone entering the church.

It's not a laughing matter, but this is…

Holy Trinity Church
Born in 1778, Joseph Grimaldi is heralded as 'the father of the modern- day clown'. Every year on the first Sunday

in February a memorial service is held for Grimaldi at the Holy Trinity Church in Dalston. The service is attended by hundreds of clowns from around the world, all dressed in full costume.

Crutched Friars

Founded in the late thirteenth century, the House of Crutched Friars was a Roman Catholic religious order based on the corner of Hart Street, just north of the Tower of London. With the friars long gone, all that remains is the Crutched Friar pub.

St Peter in Chepe

The Peter in the expression 'robbing Peter to pay Paul' is thought by some to refer to St Peter in Chepe, a former City of London church on the corner of Cheapside and Wood Street. With St Peter's sat in the shadow of St Paul's Cathedral, the 'robbing Peter' is said to refer to the theft of the church's natural light. Truth be known, the expression had been around long before the setting sun over St Paul's left St Peter in the dark, but it makes for a good story.

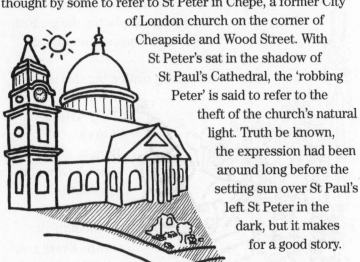

Destroyed in the Great Fire of London, all that remains of St Peter in Chepe is a small nondescript churchyard with one lone London plane tree. A bird singing in the tree inspired William Wordsworth to write the poem 'The Reverie of Poor Susan'.

St Andrew-by-the-Wardrobe

The church of St Andrew-by-the-Wardrobe in Queen Victoria Street in the City of London gained its name by its location, next to the King's Wardrobe, a store for royal ceremonial garments. The store was destroyed in 1666 in the Great Fire.

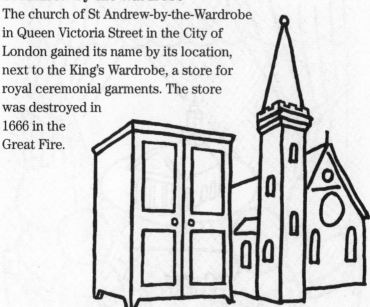

St Ann's Church

Felix Mendelssohn composed the 'Wedding March' in 1842 as part of his suite of incidental music to accompany Shakespeare's *A Midsummer Night's Dream*. Among other works, Mendelssohn gave recitals of the 'Wedding March' on the organ of St Ann's Church in south Tottenham. The organ is still in place to this day.

St Paul's Church

St Paul's Church in Covent Garden is affectionately known as the Actors' Church, having been associated with the theatre community since the opening of London's oldest theatre, the Theatre Royal in Drury Lane, in 1663.

Notable people from the acting profession remembered on memorial plaques within the church and small garden include Gracie Fields, Charlie Chaplin, Noël Coward and Boris Karloff.

St Bride's

The traditional layered wedding cake was designed in the late eighteenth century by a baker's apprentice by the name of either Thomas or William Rich; reports vary. Working in Ludgate Hill, the apprentice based his design on the steeple of St Bride's church in nearby Fleet Street. Unfortunately, as with his correct name, there are no surviving records of the cake.

Given the nature of the tale, it could be said that there is not a crumb of supporting evidence.

Chapter 4

GOD SAVE THE QUEEN

Her Majesty the Queen's underwear is made by Rigby & Peller in Hans Road, Knightsbridge.

Speaking of the Queen, one hopes one might be amused by these royal tales...

Queen Anne's Footstool

With its distinctive four corner towers, St John's in Smith Square, Westminster, is often referred to as Queen Anne's Footstool.

According to folklore, when designer Thomas Archer asked the Queen what she wanted the church to look like, she kicked over her footstool and declared, 'Like that!'

22 Charles Street

Before being crowned King William IV in 1830, the Duke of Clarence sired 10 illegitimate children with his mistress, Dorothea Jordan, at 22 Charles Street in Mayfair. The story goes that when the Duke tried to reduce her allowance, the Irish actress handed him a pile of bills, on which the attached note read: 'No money refunded after the rising of the curtain'.

The couple's great-great-great-great-great-grandson, David Cameron, later became British prime minister.

Platforms 9 and 10, King's Cross Station

In AD 60 or 61, Queen Boadicea – or Boudicca – led an uprising of indigenous tribes against the Roman invaders of Britain. Legend less reliable than an out-of-date train timetable tells that the Queen and her army were eventually defeated on the outskirts of London, at a village later to become known as Battle Bridge. Rather than fall into Roman hands, along with her three daughters, Boadicea took poison to end her life.

In 1852 King's Cross station was opened on the site of Battle Bridge, and the Queen is said to lie somewhere beneath Platforms 9 and 10.

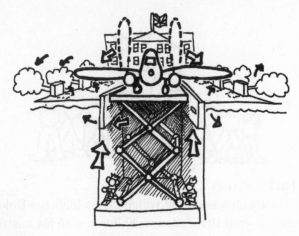

The Mall

Popular urban myth tells that in the event of an emergency
which might put the Royal Family in danger, The Mall –
the long straight road that connects Buckingham Palace
with Trafalgar Square – can rapidly be transformed into a
temporary airport runway.

The Queens Larder

While doctors in Queen Square in Bloomsbury were treating
King George III for his apparent madness, his wife, Queen
Charlotte, rented premises in the square to store and cook
his favourite food. That premises is now a pub – The Queens
Larder.

Museum of London

The Museum of London owns a pair of
Queen Victoria's undergarments.

Albert Memorial

Stood directly to the north of the Royal Albert Hall, the Albert Memorial was commissioned by Queen Victoria in memory of her beloved husband, Prince Albert. In remembrance of his involvement with the Great Exhibition of 1851, Albert is holding an Exhibition catalogue.

Diana, Princess of Wales Memorial Fountain

Unlike the beautifully ornate Trevi Fountain of Rome, the one thing the Memorial Fountain to Diana, Princess of Wales is not is a fountain. Made from 545 large pieces of Cornish granite at a cost approaching a City banker's bonus, what we have here is an extremely large oval stream bed, with water gently making its way down either side of a shallow slope.

Although not displeasing to the eye, designer Kathryn Gustafson's vision of a place to quietly wade has sadly gone wrong; not as a result of her design, but because the Cornish granite has proved as slippery as a greasy ball bearing, and soon after opening, following three cases of people performing involuntary aqua-aerobics, the fountain was closed.

Following work on the drainage, the laying of new hard surfaces and enclosure of the area with a fence, the fountain is now patrolled by wardens, preventing anyone from walking in the water or on the surrounding side walls, or undertaking any pastime that could in any way be described as pleasure.

Chapter 5

IT'S NOT THE SIZE

At its narrowest point, Narrow Street in Limehouse, East London, is the width of the combined length of two double-decker buses. It's also well over three quarters of a mile long

Perhaps it should be renamed Short Street…

Hide
With just four letters, Hide lays claim to having London's shortest street name.

Royal Albert Hall Organ
With 147 stops and 9,999 pipes, the Grand Organ in the Royal Albert Hall is the second largest pipe organ in the United Kingdom, beaten only by the 10,268 pipes of Liverpool Cathedral's Grand Organ.

**Emerald
Court**

At a buttock
clenching
67cm,
London's
narrowest
alleyway
is Emerald
Court in
Bloomsbury.

EMERALD
COURT

National Gallery Floor Mosaic

The mosaic flooring on the first-floor landing and at the top of the staircase inside the main portico entrance to the National Gallery in Trafalgar Square depicts everything and everyone, from Greta Garbo to a mud pie and a Christmas plum pudding. Consisting of over two million individual tiles, it is, quite possibly, the biggest mosaic in London.

Quite possibly, but not definitely, as – having lost count at 1,534,726 – there may be more mosaic tiles on the floor of the Arab Hall in Leighton House in Holland Park Road, Kensington.

Cabman's Shelter

On the north-west corner of Russell Square sits a small green hut with a slate roof that looks like a strong gust of wind would finish it off.

By law no bigger than a horse and cart, this Grade II listed

building is an original cabman's shelter, built in the late 1880s for the drivers of London's horse-drawn taxicabs to park up for a steaming hot brew and a chance to chew the cud with their fellow cabbies.

Of the original 61 built, the cabman's shelter in Russell Square is one of only 13 that remain.

Victorian Turkish Baths

Just south of Liverpool Street station, opposite the original Bishop's Gate to the City of London, sits St Botolph-without-Bishopsgate church. At the rear of the church garden, dwarfed by surrounding skyscrapers, nestles one of London's hidden gems. Now a restaurant, with stairs leading below ground to three tiled rooms, the diminutive folly was once a Victorian Turkish baths.

Henry Addington

Overlooking Heron Quay in Canary Wharf, the Henry Addington used to lay claim to having the longest pub bar in England. Stretching further than two bendy buses, the bar once snaked the entire length of the pub until, in 2006, several metres were removed to create an eating area.

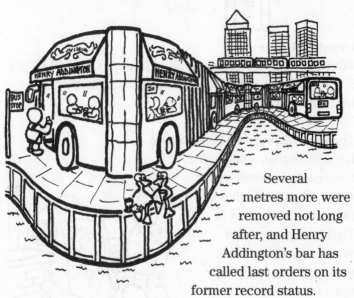

Several metres more were removed not long after, and Henry Addington's bar has called last orders on its former record status.

10 Hyde Park Place

A little over one metre in width, 10 Hyde Park Place, just west of Marble Arch, is the narrowest house in London. Thought to have been built to deter grave-robbers by blocking a passageway to the graveyard of nearby St George's church, despite its size, in 1941 the thin slither of a house was hit by a Luftwaffe bomb. It's now part of the Tyburn Convent.

Crooked Usage

Not wanting to waste a good bit of tarmac, Crooked Usage is a little bit of road left over after the straightening of Hendon Lane in Finchley.

Trafalgar Square Police Station

Little more than a bulge in a lamp post, the small round structure with a light on top in the south-east corner of Trafalgar Square is the world's smallest police station. If you can't find it, ask a policeman.

Chapter 6

THE STREETS OF LONDON

Stand on the pavement outside number 429 the Strand, look up, and you will see 18 naked male statues with their members dismembered. Originally the headquarters of the British Medical Association, the building's statues are said to represent 'The Ages of Man'.

Story tells of a man in the 1930s walking past the building when he was struck on the head by a falling stone penis. For safety, all the remaining statues had their manhoods removed.

The building is now the Zimbabwean Embassy.

Charing Cross Road
The Charing Cross Road, between Cambridge Circus and Tottenham Court Road, was originally known as Hog Lane.

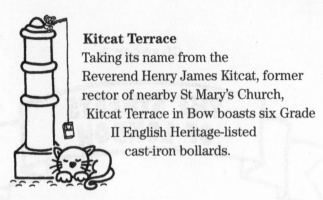

Kitcat Terrace

Taking its name from the Reverend Henry James Kitcat, former rector of nearby St Mary's Church, Kitcat Terrace in Bow boasts six Grade II English Heritage-listed cast-iron bollards.

Tweezer's Alley

Performed annually at the Royal Courts of Justice, 'the Rendering of the Quit Rents to the Crown' takes the form of two ancient ceremonies, whereby the City of London pays service for three pieces of land.

Dating from 1235, one of the pieces of land – for which the City of London must pay six horseshoes and 61 horseshoe nails – is The Forge in Tweezer's Alley, a rather nondescript passageway not far from Temple Underground station.

The origin of the passageway's name is unknown.

In the second ceremony, a quit rent of £11 is paid for the 'Town of Southwark'. Considering Southwark constitutes the majority of the south bank of the River Thames as it flows through central London, this is quite a bargain.

Electric Avenue

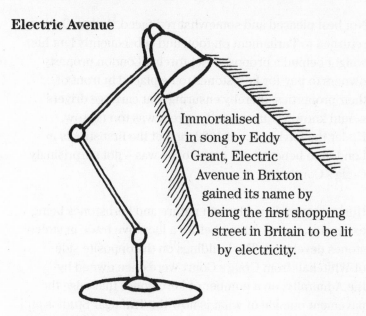

Immortalised in song by Eddy Grant, Electric Avenue in Brixton gained its name by being the first shopping street in Britain to be lit by electricity.

Craig's Court

As Speaker of the House of Commons for over two decades in the mid-eighteenth century, Arthur Onslow was a popular and well-respected politician. One day, Onslow was travelling north along Whitehall, planning to pay a visit to the Earl of Harrington. As his driver turned right into Craig's Court, just before Trafalgar Square, the Speaker's wide, stately carriage wheels became firmly wedged against the walls of the alley. Unable to open the doors and with all attempts to extricate the carriage proving fruitless, the respected politician had to be un-ceremonially removed via a hole cut in the carriage roof.

Not best pleased and somewhat red-faced, Arthur Onslow returned to Parliament on foot, and subsequently lent his weight behind a proposed Act forcing London property owners to pay for kerbstones to be placed in front of their properties, thereby ensuring that carriage drivers would know to turn back if a street was too narrow. Under the Paving Act of 1762, one of the first streets in London to benefit from kerbstones was – not surprisingly – Craig's Court.

Human nature being human nature and kerbstones being expensive, it wasn't long before a lucrative trade in stolen stones developed. The buildings on the opposite side of Whitehall from Craig's Court were once owned by the Admiralty; on a number of kerbstones that edge the pavement outside of what is now the Trafalgar Studios and The Lord Moon of The Mall pub can still be seen a faint anchor – the mark of the Admiralty – engraved into the stones in the eighteenth century to prevent the theft of army and navy property.

The Mall

Sitting atop each street lamp lining The Mall is a different ship, each one representing a vessel sunk by Admiral Lord Nelson in his naval campaigns. Meanwhile Nelson stands proud on his column in nearby Trafalgar Square, his eyes looking down on the miniature ships, his battle conquests.

Oxford Circus

Allowing shoppers to cross diagonally in an X, the £5-million pedestrian crossing at Oxford Circus was opened in 2009 by London Mayor Boris Johnson along with his grandiose declarations about it being a triumph of innovation.

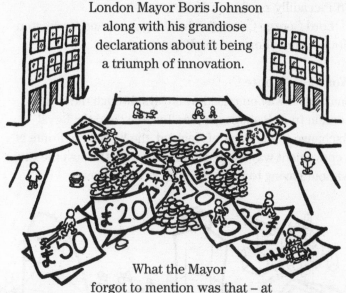

What the Mayor forgot to mention was that – at considerably less cost – a similar pedestrian crossing had been opened in Balham, south-west London four years earlier.

Burlington Arcade

The story goes that whenever Lord George Cavendish attempted to relax in his Burlington House garden he would find himself bombarded by everything from oyster shells to the occasional dead cat, tossed over the wall by passers-by using the alleyway running

43

alongside his garden. The solution was obvious: pay for
an arcade of shops to be built, enclosing the alleyway. The
result: Burlington Arcade, a row of tiny Georgian shops just
off Piccadilly, opened in 1819.

Lord George Cavendish has long gone, and Burlington
House is now home to the Royal Academy.

Wormhole Route
Snaking its way on raised walkways through the City of
London from Bishopsgate, via Tower 42 and the Royal
Exchange to the Bank of England, the Wormhole Route is
a convenient way for pedestrians to walk through the City
without having to cross the busy streets below.

Ha-Ha Road

Ha-Ha Road in Woolwich follows the path of the ha-ha – a hidden wall with a grassy slope – that separates the Royal Artillery Barrack Field from Woolwich Common. The ha-ha was built around 1774 to stop sheep and cattle straying onto the gunnery range.

And just for a laugh, the ha-ha is to be found on English Heritage's *Statutory List of Buildings of Special Architectural or Historic Interest*. Not bad for a wall.

_Quaggy Walk

Rising in Sundridge Park, running through four parks and a golf course before joining the River Ravensbourne in Lewisham, the River Quaggy is one of London's

lesser-known rivers. Gaining its name from the word 'quagmire', the River Quaggy is, as you might guess, prone to severe flooding.

Quaggy Walk, when not underwater, follows the path of the river.

Chiswick Flyover

Not so much a street as a big road, the Chiswick Flyover – part of the Great West Road into London – was officially opened in 1959 by Hollywood actress Jayne Mansfield.

Ely Place

Pass through the entrance gates into Ely Place – just off Holborn Circus in the City of London – and you will find yourself in the county of Cambridgeshire. Originally home to the Bishop of Ely when visiting the capital on ministerial business, the tiny Cambridgeshire enclave is off limits to City of London police, who are forbidden to enter without first seeking permission from the commissioner of the street's elected governing body.

The county border runs through the local pub – Ye Olde Mitre tavern – whose licensing hours were, until the 1960s, under the jurisdiction of Cambridgeshire authorities.

South Audley Street

If you look in the window of West One Bathrooms in South Audley Street, Mayfair, you just might see a gold bath, a marble washbasin with a price tag in excess of £450,000 and a naked female statue toilet with a gold seat.

Chapter 7

BLOTS ON THE LONDON LANDSCAPE

Made from dark beige Brazilian marble, 39 Tite Street in Chelsea may win my own personal award for the ugliest structure in London. Pop on your dark glasses and seek out a few of the other contenders...

No. 1 Poultry

Replacing the much-loved Mappin and Webb building in the City of London, No. 1 Poultry is a post modern building that tried hard to be something but didn't achieve the correct grades. The unpleasant salmon-coloured exterior hides an open interior triangle core that looks like it was constructed by a group of three-year-olds from giant toy building blocks, with a coat of high-gloss varnish added by the parents to preserve their precious offspring's first efforts.

Crystal Palace Park Concert Platform

A 25-metre-wide sheet of rusting metal resting on the edge of a small lake in a dip surrounded by trees, Crystal Palace Park Concert Platform is a blot on the rolling landscape best reserved for a scrap-metal dealer.

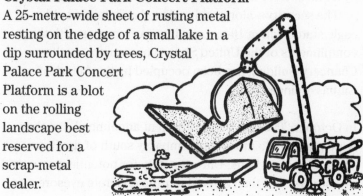

To add insult to eyesore, the concert platform – referred to by locals as the 'rusty laptop' – rarely appears to stage any concerts.

Chancery Building

Designed in the Brutalist style of architecture – the name originating from the French *béton brut*, meaning 'raw concrete' – the Chancery Building covers the entire west side of Grosvenor Square, Mayfair. At least six floors above ground and as big as a football pitch, the building is as brutally ugly as it sounds. Luckily for the rest of the residents in the square, the building is partially hidden by a line of trees and a cordon of high-level security.

The security – along with a gilded aluminium bald-eagle statue with a 10-metre wingspan – comes with the compliments of the United States government, as the Chancery Building has been occupied by the American Embassy since 1960.

In October 2008, the US government announced that they were planning to move their embassy south of the River Thames to Nine Elms. Unfortunately for potential property developers, less than a year later the concrete eyesore was granted Grade II listed protection status.

Southbank Centre
Rich pickings for London's culture-vultures, the construction of what was at first called the South Bank Centre – comprising the Royal Festival Hall, Queen Elizabeth Hall, Purcell Room and Hayward Art Gallery – began in 1949, two years before the Festival of Britain. With an apparent lack of quick-drying cement, building work wasn't finally completed until 1968.

Renamed the Southbank Centre, since the new millennium the now ageing and water-stained concrete blot on London's landscape has undergone a cosmetic makeover in an attempt to make it more pleasing to the eye, with raised pedestrian walkways removed and shops and restaurants added, along with a liberal use of glass and coloured lighting.

Michael Faraday Memorial

Sat in the middle of the northern traffic island at Elephant and Castle is a large stainless steel box. Possibly the ugliest piece of outdoor artwork in London, the oversized sardine can was built in honour of famed electrochemist Michael Faraday, who was born nearby in Newington Butts.

Fittingly, given that Faraday is known for his early experimentation with electricity, the box also contains an electrical substation for the nearby Northern Line.

Fulcrum

On the corner of the western entrance to Liverpool Street station stands Fulcrum, a 'minimalist work of art' by Richard Serra. Four rusty sheets of steel rising up the height of three double-decker buses, Fulcrum is best described as an eyesore.

Four fewer sheets would be an improvement.

Barbican Centre

The largest performing-arts centre in Europe, the Barbican
Centre is part of the Barbican Estate, built post-Second
World War to fill a large hole in the City of London caused
by Luftwaffe bombs. With its open windy raised walkways
and liberal misuse of now stained and ageing concrete,
the Barbican Estate is to architecture what a fast-food
restaurant is to fine cuisine.

Despite undergoing a number of makeovers in an attempt to
disguise the blot on the landscape, as the saying goes, you
can't make a silk purse out of a pig's ear, and the Barbican
Centre is considered by many to be London's ugliest building.

Section 2

CULTURE VULTURE

Chapter 8

MUSEUM PIECE

From dentistry to Dalí, sewage to Saatchi, London boasts more than 240 museums.

Time to blow the dust off a few display cabinets…

Natural History Museum
The oldest thing on the entire planet – meteorite dust – is to be found in a small glass phial in The Vault gallery of the Natural History Museum in Kensington. Formed over 4,567 million years ago, the dust is older than our solar system.

Horniman Museum

Opened in Forest Hill in 1901 to house tea merchant Frederick John Horniman's collection of – among other things – natural history, the Horniman Museum's most famous exhibit is the stuffed walrus.

Given nothing but a walrus's skin and not knowing at the time what a walrus looked like, in 1870 a Canadian taxidermist stuffed the skin to its limits, creating an over-inflated balloon with a pair of tusks, not far short of the size of a small car.

Clink Prison Museum

Situated next to the remains of the Bishop of Winchester's Palace (I use the word 'remains' lightly, as we're talking around 25 bricks, an old window frame and enough scaffold poles to stretch the length of the River Thames), the Clink Prison – opened in 1151 – was notorious in its day, locking up anyone and everyone, be they Protestant, Catholic, priest or a prostitute from one of the many local brothels.

Knowing the reputation of the medieval clergy, it's likely that priests and prostitutes were often arrested at the same time.

55

Clink prisoners were not only subjected to torture and beheading; they also had to pay for their own keep. One can only presume the final bill would be settled before head removal.

Aside from its brutal conditions, the Clink is most famous as the origin of the expression 'in the clink', meaning 'in prison', coming from both its location in Clink Street and the clinking sound of the manacles and leg irons.

Despite recreating the scene of a beheading using a wooden block and a rubber axe, walls painted to look old covered in stuff to read about prison life, and examples of various forms of torture – from the chastity belt to listening to improvised jazz – the problem with being 'in the clink' is that you're not actually *in* the Clink: the Clink Prison was razed to the ground during the Gordon Riots of 1780 and never rebuilt. The Clink Prison Museum is actually the basement of a former warehouse.

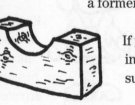

If you're interested in rubber axes, I'd suggest a joke shop.

Design Museum

Whatever the exhibition, be it
'Postmodernist Camping
Equipment' or 'Iconic
Twentieth Century Cutlery',
around 75 per cent of all
objects on display at the
Design Museum in Shad
Thames appear, for some
reason, to be chairs: inflatable
chairs, wooden chairs, metal chairs,
plastic chairs, stacking chairs, armchairs, garden chairs,
high chairs, low chairs…every chair you can imagine.

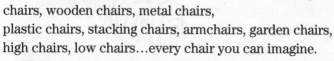

With more chairs than the chair department of a well-known Swedish furniture store, the Design Museum should really be renamed the Chair Museum.

At the time of writing, plans are afoot (or perhaps that should be a-leg, given the nature of the exhibits) for the Design Museum to up furniture and move to the former Commonwealth Institute building in Kensington.

British Optical Association Museum

Barely the toss of a monocle lens from
Trafalgar Square, the British Optical
Association Museum in Craven Street
boasts more than 11,000 objects
relating to the history of optometry,
including glasses with battery-operated
windscreen wipers and the
spectacles of famed wife-
murderer, Dr Crippen.

Grant Museum of Zoology

Founded in 1828 by Robert Grant, the first professor of zoology at the University of London and mentor to the young Charles Darwin, the Grant Museum of Zoology is a fascinating collection of around 67,000 animal specimens, with glass cases displaying everything from a pickled hedgehog, an elephant heart and a walrus penis bone, to the skeletons of an aye-aye, anaconda snake, donkey, warthog, spotted hyena and aardwolf, along with the extinct dodo, quagga and Tasmanian tiger.

Far more dangerous than the Tasmanian tiger, the collection also houses some fine specimens of the world's most dangerous of creatures – *Homo sapiens*.

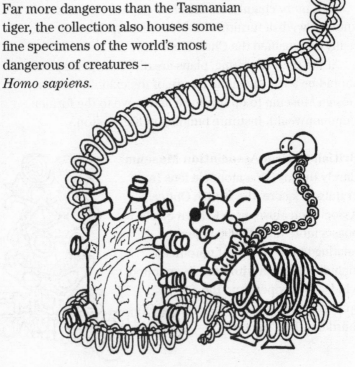

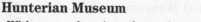

Hunterian Museum

With more glass jars than a jam-making factory, the thousands of anatomical specimens and medical curiosities on display at the Hunterian Museum – housed in the headquarters of the Royal College of Surgeons of England in Lincoln's Inn Fields – include pickled tumours, malignant melanomas, warts, hernias, the pickled foot of an elephantiasis patient, and a large cyst removed from a woman's chin.

Museum of London

With more than 17,000 skeletons in its collection, the Museum of London has over three times the number of dead bodies than a full capacity audience at the Royal Albert Hall.

MCC Museum

Within the boundary of
Lord's Cricket Ground in
St John's Wood, the MCC
Museum has on display
both a stuffed sparrow
and the cricket ball that
it failed to avoid.

Kew Bridge Steam Museum

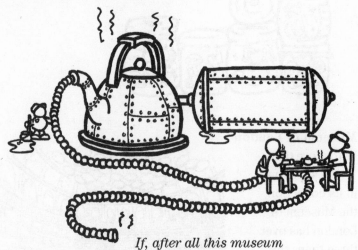

*If, after all this museum
visiting, you're in need
of a cup of tea, Kew
Bridge Steam Museum
is never short of
hot water.*

Chapter 9

ALL THE WORLD'S A STAGE

When William Shakespeare wrote 'All the world's a stage, and all the men and women merely players', he wasn't expecting a pair of dolphins…

Peacock Theatre
During the 1970s, Paul Raymond, renowned owner of the Raymond Revuebar strip club in Soho, staged revue shows at the Peacock Theatre in Portugal Street. During a performance known as *The Great International Nude Show*, a large water tank containing two dolphins would be raised up to the stage. After performing a number of tricks, one of the dolphins would then remove the bra from 'Miss Nude International'.

Watery legend tells that the dolphins were left to die of neglect, and, for many years, ghostly squeals could be heard from below the stage…

On more solid ground, until Aldwych Underground station closed in 1994, trains ran directly below the theatre and the 'crying baby' sounds were most likely the squeak of distant wheels. The two dolphins, named Pixie and Penny, were in fact relocated to the dolphinarium at Woburn Safari Park.

Meanwhile, the Peacock Theatre moved on from dolphins unclipping bras to becoming the studio for the TV programme *This Is Your Life*. However, part of the water tank and its lifting gear are still to be found beneath the stage.

Wood Green Empire
Famed for his bullet-catching-between-the-teeth trick, on 23 March 1918, magician Chung Ling Soo met his end on stage at the Wood Green Empire, when he failed to catch a bullet. The auditorium has since been demolished to make way for a multistorey car park, but the façade – in the centre of a row of shops on Wood Green High Road – is still visible.

> TOUPÉE OR NOT TOUPÉE

Savoy Theatre
Remembered for his role in *Ben-Hur* and many other Hollywood epics, the story is told that when veteran actor Charlton Heston appeared in *A Man for All Seasons* at the Savoy Theatre in 1987, he was called upon to wear a wig. Rather than admit to the theatre's make-up department that he already wore a wig (despite the fact

being widely known), he appeared on stage wearing a wig on top of his wig.

Playhouse Theatre

On the corner of Craven Street and Northumberland Avenue, the auditorium of the Playhouse Theatre sits below the suspended platforms of Charing Cross station. When, during repairs to the station in 1905, a faulty weld in a tierod gave way, a large section of roof, together with part of the western wall, collapsed, crashing through to what was then the Royal Avenue Theatre below, killing three people on the station and injuring others in the theatre.

Although the theatre has since been rebuilt, when attending a performance you may wish to remember that heavy trains are sitting directly above you on suspended platforms and, as passengers board, they gradually become heavier...

259 Whitechapel Road

Joseph 'John' Merrick, better known due to his 'elephant-like' deformities as the 'Elephant Man', was exhibited at the back of an empty shop at 259 Whitechapel Road. He later lived in the east wing of the Royal London Hospital in Whitechapel. In 1987, singer Michael Jackson allegedly offered the London Hospital Medical College one million dollars for Merrick's remains. The college turned down the offer.

Little Theatre

There are a number of theories as to the origin of the expression 'Break a leg!' – used to wish someone luck before a performance. One popular suggestion is that it originates from what was the Little Theatre in Haymarket. The bones of the story involve theatre owner Samuel Foote, the Duke of York and a horse.

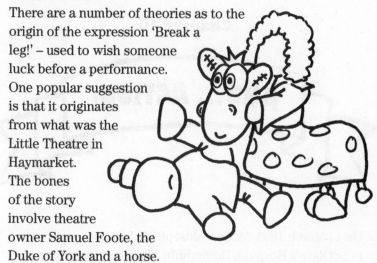

Following the incident, the Little Theatre gained its theatrical licence and – receiving the Royal Warrant of approval – changed its name to the Theatre Royal.

If you would like to hear the story in greater detail, ask the person at the box office. I'm sure they'll be pleased to help, especially five minutes before a performance.

Chapter 10

AND... ACTION!

On 14 March 1933, Maurice Joseph Micklewhite was born in St Olave's Hospital, Rotherhithe. The story goes that, looking for a more memorable acting stage name, while speaking to his agent from a Leicester Square telephone kiosk, Micklewhite noticed that the 1954 film *The Caine Mutiny* was showing at the nearby Odeon cinema. Changing his name to Michael Caine, the much-loved actor has since gone on to appear in over 100 films...

Crystal Palace Park Athletics Track
After witnessing the blowing up of an old white van in the original 1969 film version of *The Italian Job*, Michael Caine's character famously exclaims: 'You're only supposed to blow the bloody doors off!' The quote was voted one of the all-time great movie one-liners.

With Crystal Palace Park's television mast clearly visible in the background, the scene was filmed inside the park's athletics track.

Acton Lane Power Station
With metal-grille walkways and long corridors, Acton Lane Power Station in Ealing has proved a popular film location. Generating its last megawatt of electricity in 1983, in 1986 the interior of the disused power station was used for the 'Alien nest' scenes in the film *Aliens*.

Left in place after filming, the set reappeared as the Axis Chemical Plant in the 1989 film *Batman*, with Jack Nicholson's character Jack Napier seen to plunge into a boiling vat, only to return as 'The Joker'.

Leighton House
The gilt-and-blue Islamic tiled interior of the Arab Hall in Leighton House, Holland Park Road, doubled as the plastic surgery clinic in the 1985 film, *Brazil*.

Beckton Gasworks

With director Stanley Kubrick not wishing to leave Britain, battle scenes in the Vietnamese war epic *Full Metal Jacket* were filmed among the dynamited ruins of Beckton gasworks. Palm trees were imported from Spain to recreate a South Asian landscape.

The opening helicopter action sequence of the Bond film *For Your Eyes Only* and the Lunghua Camp scenes in Steven Spielberg's *Empire of the Sun* were also shot at what was once Europe's largest gasworks.

New Concordia Wharf

The flat where Archie was dangled from the window in *A Fish Called Wanda* was located in New Concordia Wharf, between Shad Thames and Mill Street in Bermondsey.

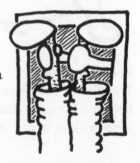

Croydon B Power Station

The imposing entrance to Croydon B Power Station doubled as the exterior of the infamous Ministry in Terry Gilliam's 1985 film, *Brazil*. The interior of one of the giant cooling towers also doubled as the torture chamber.

Having been decommissioned the previous year, Croydon B Power Station has since been demolished and is now an IKEA store. All that remains are the twin towers, ringed in blue and yellow neon and standing proud in the self-assembly furniture store car park. The surrounding street names of Ampere, Volta and Galvani hold testament to the former power station.

The Globe
Bridget's flat in the 2001 film *Bridget Jones's Diary* was situated above The Globe pub in Bedale Street, Southwark.

Duke of Albany

In the spoof zombie film *Shaun of the Dead*, Shaun and his mates take refuge in The Winchester pub. The scenes were filmed in the Duke of Albany in Monson Road, New Cross.
The pub has since been converted into flats.

Fulham Broadway Underground Station

In the 1998 film *Sliding Doors*, Helen Quilley's future is determined by whether she makes it on-board a train before the doors close. The scene, starring Gwyneth Paltrow, was filmed at Fulham Broadway Underground station.

All Saints Fulham

In the 1976 film *The Omen*, Father Brennan met his end, speared by a flagpole falling from the spire of a church.
The scene was filmed in the graveyard of All Saints Church, Fulham.

St Michael and All Angels Church

The St Michael and All Angels church in Turnham Green appeared as the exterior of the convent in the 1990 British comedy, *Nuns on the Run*.

St Bartholomew the Great

The wedding where Charles doesn't marry 'Duckface' Henrietta in *Four Weddings and a Funeral* was filmed at St Bartholomew the Great in Kinghorn Street, Smithfield.

A popular film location, the church can also be seen in *Robin Hood: Prince of Thieves*; *Shakespeare in Love* and the 2009 film, *Sherlock Holmes*.

142 Portobello Road

William Thacker's travel bookshop in the film *Notting Hill* was at 142 Portobello Road. The shop was based on a real travel bookshop around the corner at 13–15 Blenheim Crescent.

Brompton Cemetery

Both the sequence outside of the Russian church in the 1995 Bond film *GoldenEye* and the scene where Rowan Atkinson disrupts a funeral in the 2003 Bond spoof *Johnny English* were filmed in Brompton Cemetery.

The Victorian cemetery was also the setting for Lord Blackwood's mysterious resurrection from the family vault in Guy Ritchie's 2009 film, *Sherlock Holmes*.

Millwall Dock

Parts of the jet-boat chase sequence in the James Bond film *The World Is Not Enough* were filmed in Millwall Dock on the Isle of Dogs. Bond, in his 'Q' boat, is seen to dive underwater to avoid the closing bascules of Glengall Bridge.

Lawrence Hall

The grand art deco interior of Lawrence Hall in Greycoat Street, Westminster, appeared as Berlin Airport in the 1989 film, *Indiana Jones and the Last Crusade*.

42 Bull's Head Passage

A fourteenth-century covered market in the City of London, Leadenhall Market played a starring role in the first Harry Potter film, with Bull's Head Passage transformed into Diagon Alley, the wizard shopping street where Harry Potter searches for his magic wand in the 2001 film, *Harry Potter and the Philosopher's Stone*. Number 42 Bull's Head Passage appeared as the entrance to the Leaky Cauldron, the pub serving as a gateway between Diagon Alley and the non-wizard 'muggle' street of Charing Cross Road.

Tooting Bec Lido

Measuring 90 by 30 metres, Tooting Bec Lido is the largest open-air pool in Europe.

With a plot involving stolen diamonds and a small-time boxing promoter, the lido appears in Guy Ritchie's 2000 film, *Snatch*.

Chapter 11

TV OR NOT TV

In January 1926, John Logie Baird gave the first public demonstration of his new invention – television – from his flat on the top floor of 22 Frith Street.

Press the red button on your remote now…

Cardinal Cap Alley

Known in the sixteenth century as Cardinal's Hat Alley, Cardinal Cap Alley – on the south bank of the River Thames, looking across to St Paul's Cathedral – features in the *Doctor Who* episode *The Talons of Weng-Chiang*.

Sandwiched between the Tate Modern and Shakespeare's Globe Theatre, it's believed that the alley gained its unusual name from once leading to an inn or brothel called the Cardinal's Hat.

74

Florin Court

Whitehaven Mansions, seen on TV as the home
of Belgian private detective Hercule Poirot,
was in reality Florin Court, a curvy art
deco building in Charterhouse Square in
Smithfield. In filming the building for the
TV series, the cameras were positioned
to avoid capturing either Lauderdale
or Shakespeare Tower, both part of the
Barbican Estate (see page 52).

The view of the two
brutally unpleasant 42-storey
concrete tower blocks
overshadowing the historic
square is enough to have
the countless victims of
the Black Death, buried in
Charterhouse Square in 1348,
turning in their mass grave.

1–4 Jacob's Well Mews

Many animated children's television favourites, including
Parsley the Lion, *The Herbs*, *Hattytown*, *Paddington Bear*
and *The Wombles*, along with lesser-known series like
Moschops and *Portland Bill*, were produced by a company
called FilmFair, based at 1–4 Jacob's Well Mews, just off
Marylebone High Street.

The series were filmed in a small studio behind the old
stable doors in the mews and nearby at 45 Blandford Street.
Although the original Blandford Street façade is still intact,
the studio has since been demolished and redeveloped as
Admiral Court.

58 Queen's Gate Mews

The original series of the animated children's TV series, *Postman Pat*, was filmed in a small studio behind the stable doors of 58 Queen's Gate Mews in Kensington.

Wood Green Bus Garage

The popular seventies TV sitcom *On the Buses* was filmed in the Eastern National bus garage in Wood Green. The garage, on Lordship Lane, has since been demolished.

Harlech Tower

On the South Acton Estate in Ealing, Harlech Tower doubled as the exterior of Nelson Mandela House, Peckham home to Rodney and Del Boy Trotter in the long-running TV comedy *Only Fools and Horses*.

Earmarked for demolition, the ageing concrete tower has since earned a reprieve, having instead been clad in white panels.

55 Kewferry Road

On the day of his fortieth birthday, draftsman Tom Good convinces his wife Barbara that it's time to change their hectic lifestyle and embark upon a self-sufficient suburban one, tending chickens and pigs and growing their own food in the back garden.

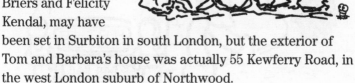

The 1970s TV sitcom *The Good Life*, starring Richard Briers and Felicity Kendal, may have been set in Surbiton in south London, but the exterior of Tom and Barbara's house was actually 55 Kewferry Road, in the west London suburb of Northwood.

24 Oil Drum Lane

Rag-and-bone merchants Albert and Harold Steptoe, of the hit TV sitcom *Steptoe and Son*, lived at 24 Oil Drum Lane, a fictional address in Shepherd's Bush.

Lapstone Gardens

It's Gourmet Night at the Fawlty Towers hotel. Basil Fawlty is driving back from André's restaurant with a duck. He turns the corner, only to find his way blocked by a van. Reversing onto the pavement, the engine of the battered old Austin 1300 finally splutters to a halt. Rather than wait for roadside assistance, Basil Fawlty gets out, picks up the fallen branch of a tree, and gives the car 'a damn good thrashing'.

One of the most famous scenes from the TV sitcom *Fawlty Towers*, the sequence was filmed at the T-junction of Lapstone Gardens and Mentmore Close in Kenton.

Chapter 12

OWL-STRETCHING TIME

Suggested names for what was to become the cult comedy TV series *Monty Python's Flying Circus* included *Bun, Whackett, Buzzard, Stubble and Boot*; *Owl-Stretching Time*; and *A Horse, a Bucket and a Spoon*.

And now for something else completely useless…

Thorpebank Road
The 'Gas Cooker', the 'Seduced Milkman' and the start of the 'Ministry of Silly Walks' sketches were all filmed in Thorpebank Road, Hammersmith.

Hurlingham Park

Fulham's Hurlingham Park was the setting for 'Upper Class Twit of the Year', a Python sketch that involved an obstacle course race between five upper-class twits.

71 Fenchurch Street

In Terry Gilliam's 'Crimson Permanent Assurance' sketch, the elderly employees of a London assurance firm rebel against a take-over from the Very Big Corporation of America by turning their office building into a pirate ship and sailing through the City of London. The short film – screened in cinemas at the start of *Monty Python's The Meaning of Life* – was filmed at 71 Fenchurch Street.

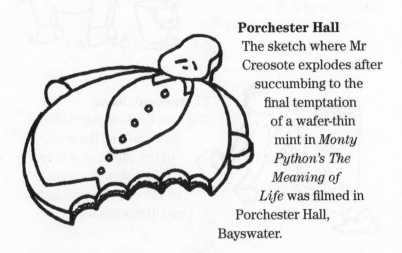

Porchester Hall

The sketch where Mr Creosote explodes after succumbing to the final temptation of a wafer-thin mint in *Monty Python's The Meaning of Life* was filmed in Porchester Hall, Bayswater.

Teddington Lock

Teddington Lock, the last River Thames crossing within the western boundary of Greater London, was used as the location for the 'Fish Slapping Dance', a sketch featuring John Cleese and Michael Palin. The sketch ends with Michael Palin falling into the lock, having been slapped by an oversized fish.

Chapter 13

ALL CREATURES GREAT AND SMALL

The most common occupant of Trafalgar Square was not always the tourist: until recent times it was the feral pigeon. Before the feeding of pigeons in the square was banned in 2001, the notorious disease-carrying birds – at the time numbering 4,000 – deposited enough excrement per year on Nelson's Column and local buildings to fill more than 500 wheelie bins.

Any remaining pigeons that think they can eke out a living pecking on discarded junk food now risk becoming breakfast themselves, as the Greater London Authority employs a Harris hawk to keep an eagle-eye on the square every morning.

From Harry the Harris hawk to an ex-parrot, it's time for some furry and feathery tails...

Rossetti's Menagerie

Without doubt, the prize for London's most nuisance neighbour goes to poet Dante Gabriel Rossetti. From 1862–82, while living at 16 Cheyne Walk in Chelsea, Rossetti kept a menagerie of exotic animals that included wombats, kangaroos, armadillos, a llama, a toucan and a large black bear.

Tower of London

A nineteenth-century zoo within the walls of the Tower of London stocked mainly animals beginning with the letter 'L' – lions, leopards and lynxes. Admission was either 1½ pence or free with the donation of a cat or dog to feed to the lions.

The zoo may have long gone but the Tower of London is still home to six ravens (plus one spare, ready to step in should a raven go missing).

And go missing one did when, in 1981, after 21 years of 'service to The Crown', a raven by the name of Grog escaped and was last seen two miles away outside the Rose and Punchbowl pub in Stepney; not a bad feat considering its wings had been clipped.

Receiving more than a clip round the wings, in 1986 a raven called George was given its marching orders for 'conduct unsatisfactory' – the 'conduct' being the eating of television cables.

Legend tells that if all six ravens were to ever leave the Tower of London, the White Tower will collapse, a great disaster will befall the United Kingdom and the monarchy will perish. The ravens (and the Kingdom) did almost perish during the Second World War, when all but one raven died from shock during bombing raids.

Kaspar the Cat

Whenever a party of 13 dinner guests sits down to dine at the Savoy Hotel, the unlucky number is raised to 14 by

Kaspar, a one-metre-tall black cat carved from wood.

Suitably dressed with napkin, Kaspar is seated at the table and served each dish at the same time as the other guests.

Giro the Nazi Dog

When Giro, the faithful pet of Dr Leopold von Hoesch, the German Ambassador in London during the rise of the Nazi Party in the 1930s, died after chewing through an electrical cable in 1934, he was afforded a full Nazi burial. The message on his small headstone – sheltered under a tree between the Duke of York Steps and a ramp leading to a garage under 6–9 Carlton House Terrace – reads: *'Giro: Ein treuer Begleiter'* – 'Giro: A true companion'.

The Philpot Lane Mice

Just below the parapet, on the left pillar of the building on the south-east corner of Philpot Lane and Eastcheap, barely a stone's throw from The Monument to the Great Fire of London, is a life-sized sculpture of two mice, fighting over a piece of cheese. This is thought to be the smallest piece of permanent public art in London.

Legend tells that, during the building's construction in 1862, a workman found the cheese missing from his lunchtime sandwich. Pointing the cheesy finger of suspicion at his fellow worker, an argument ensued and, during the row, one of the workmen fell to his death. When it was later discovered that mice were the culprit, and in remembrance of the event, the sculpture was added to the building's facia.

Zebras

An avid collector of specimens for his private zoological museum, Walter Rothschild amassed a collection that included 200,000 birds' eggs, over two million butterflies and enough creatures to fill an ugly-bug ball several times over, along with various animals from all four corners of the spherical world.

In an effort to prove that certain animals could be tamed, in 1895 Rothschild drove a carriage harnessed to three zebras (and a horse to even out the numbers) along The Mall to Buckingham Palace.

Winchester Geese

As part of the Bishop of Winchester's estate, the area of Southwark bordering the south bank of the River Thames west of London Bridge was to become known as 'The Liberty of the Clink'. Licensed by the Bishop to work within the Liberty, prostitutes became known – either for the white aprons they wore or for the whiteness of their naked breasts – as 'Winchester Geese'.

Covent Garden Elephants

East of Covent Garden Piazza, 27–29 Endell Street has a wide entrance as it was built to house elephants when the circus came to town. Since the circus has long since left town, 27–29 Endell Street has more recently housed a restaurant, cabaret and cocktail bar by the name of…Circus.

Crystal Palace Dinosaurs

A mere hop, skip and jump from Crystal Palace Park's athletics track, set in among the paths and trees around a lake, brings you to Dinosaur Court – heralded at the time of opening as the 'world's first theme park'.

Commissioned in 1852, to mark the unveiling of the world's first dinosaur sculptures to an eagerly awaiting public, on New Year's Eve 1853, designer and sculptor Benjamin Waterhouse Hawkins held a dinner inside the mould of an iguanodon.

The Jungle Book

Author Rudyard Kipling worked on *The Jungle Book* while staying at Brown's Hotel in Dover Street, Mayfair.

Now known as the Kipling Suite, it's thought that author Stephen King wrote the story outline for *Misery* from the same room.

Chimps' Tea Party

It's said that, one afternoon in January 1951 during one of the regularly held chimps' tea parties, a chimpanzee escaped from London Zoo and boarded a passing number 53 bus from Plumstead to Hampstead.

Pink Inflatable Pig

The cover of the 1977 Pink Floyd album *Animals* features a pink inflatable pig flying above Battersea Power Station.

The story goes that on the day of the photo shoot the nine-metre-diameter pig broke free from its moorings, causing disruption as wind blew it across Heathrow Airport's flight path.

BEEP! BEEP!

The pig was later recovered from a field in Kent but, after a further day of filming in bad weather, the finished album cover was created using a composite of two photos.

Ye Olde Cheshire Cheese Parrot

Tucked away on Wine Office Court – a narrow alleyway off Fleet Street – Ye Olde Cheshire Cheese pub has, in its bar, a stuffed parrot.

POP! POP! POP! POP! POP! POP! POP! POP! POP! POP! SQUAWK!

As the pub celebrated victory at the end of the Great War, Polly the parrot was said to have spent an entire hour imitating the sound of champagne corks popping until, exhausted, she squawked no more.

She was, in the words of Monty Python, an ex-parrot.

Well, not quite: after regaining her breath, Polly went on to live to the grand old parrot-age of 40; her eventual passing in 1926 was reported on both BBC Radio and in newspaper obituaries the world over.

Chapter 14

GAME, SET AND MATCH

On 9 May 1770, almost two centuries before Roger Bannister became the first athlete to officially record a sub-four-minute mile, it's said that a James Parrott set off from the wall of Charterhouse, just north of Glasshouse Yard in Goswell Road, Clerkenwell. Crossing the road, Parrott headed east along Old Street, reaching the gates of St Leonard's Church in Shoreditch High Street – a distance of one mile – in exactly four minutes. For his efforts, the fruit seller won a wager of 15 guineas.

A century having passed since the invention of the chronometer, within a pace or two the measurement could be relied upon for accuracy. Nevertheless, taking place long before the existence of any official sports governing body, Parrott's achievement was neither recorded nor recognised.

Speaking of running…

White City Stadium
On 24 July 1908, London staged its first Olympic marathon. Starting from the East Terrace of Windsor Castle in

Berkshire, the course ran 26 miles to White City Stadium in west London. Entering the stadium by the south-west corner, 385 yards were added so that the competitors could circle the athletics track and cross the finish line directly below the Royal Box. And so it was that London's 1908 Olympic marathon defined the 26 miles and 385 yards (41.195km) distance standard for all modern marathons.

The race itself proved controversial: on a boiling-hot summer's day, the competitors – overdressed in heavy clothes that fitted the regulation dress code of the day – received en-route refreshment of either hot or cold OXO, with accompanying rice pudding.

Italian Dorando Pietri, the first to enter the stadium, exhausted and dehydrated, promptly collapsed. Helped to his feet by officials, Pietri staggered to the finish line, only to be disqualified for having received assistance.

White City Stadium was demolished in 1985 and the site – until 2013 – occupied by the BBC, but the finish line to the length-defining, controversial marathon is marked by a line across – appropriately – Dorando Close.

Twickenham Rugby Stadium

In April 1974, Australian Michael O'Brien became the first known streaker at a major sporting event, when he ran across the pitch naked as England played France at Twickenham rugby stadium. As he was escorted off the pitch, a policeman famously covered O'Brien's 'assets' with his helmet.

In another police cover-up, during the half-time break at an England versus Australia match in January 1982, Erica Roe and friend Sarah Bennett ran across the Twickenham pitch topless. As both were escorted off, while Bennett's modesty was hidden behind a Union Jack flag, a police officer famously attempted to hide Roe's ample bosom with his helmet. The semi-naked frolic has gone down in history as perhaps the most famous of all streaks.

Pickles the Dog, Stamps and the Football World Cup

On 27 March 1966, a dog by the name of Pickles discovered the Jules Rimet Trophy – otherwise known as the Football World Cup – concealed in newspaper under a hedge in the garden at St Valery, a large house on Beulah Hill in Norwood. The famous trophy had been stolen the previous week from a stamp exhibition in Westminster Hall.

England went on to win the World Cup four months later. While the team celebrated post-match in their changing rooms, as a precaution to ensure that there could be no possibility of a repeat theft, unbeknown to the players the trophy was cleverly swapped, and the World Cup displayed around the country for the next four years was actually a replica.

Wembley Stadium

Home to England's national football team, since reopening in 2007 after an £800-million rebuild, the new pitch at Wembley Stadium – almost four metres lower than the original pitch – has had to be relaid up to seven times a year.

According to a common tale, Wembley's drainage problems could well be a result of construction work on the original stadium in 1923, when one of the steam trains being used to transport landfill material is said to have derailed and fallen into the big hole that had been dug for the stadium's foundations.

Rather than incur the time loss and expense of removing it, so legend goes, the train was buried and – to this day – still lies beneath the Wembley pitch.

Uxbridge Cricket Club

On 21 July 2010, what was thought to be the first known meteorite to hit the UK in 20 years landed just inside the boundary line of Uxbridge Cricket Club. Breaking in two, the meteorite bounced, hitting a nearby fan in the chest.

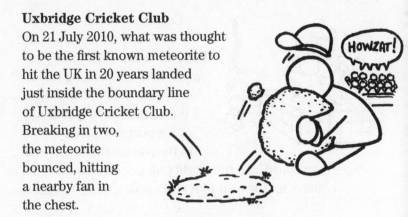

Later tests revealed the 'meteorite' to be a piece of Portland cement debris that had fallen from the undercarriage of an overflying plane. Given tales of planes jettisoning the contents of their toilets mid-air, it could've been a lot worse.

University Boat Race

Over an internationally recognised course distance of four miles and 374 yards (6.779km), the University Boat Race is battled out each spring along the banks of the River Thames between two teams of rowers from the Universities of Oxford and Cambridge. With only the two teams competing,

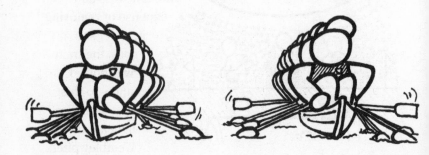

in 1949 radio commentator John Snagge, unable to see which team was ahead, famously announced that it was either Oxford or Cambridge.

The course having no winning posts or clear finishing line, in 1877 race marshal John Phelps is said to have declared the race 'a deadheat to Oxford by five feet'.

The Serpentine Christmas Day Swimming Race

Every Christmas Day morning since 1864, a large gathering of hardy souls clad in little more than goose pimples and non-obligatory Santa hats have braved freezing cold temperatures to compete in a 100-yard swimming race in the Serpentine, the large lake in Hyde Park. The winner of the race is awarded the Peter Pan Cup, donated in 1913 by *Peter Pan* author James Barrie. Barrie lived nearby in Bayswater and often walked in Kensington Gardens and Hyde Park.

Unless it's your usual attire, there's little point in turning up in skimpy Speedos, as the annual Serpentine Christmas Day Swimming Race is only open to members of the Serpentine Swimming Club.

Personally, I'd rather chew my own leg off.

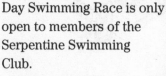

Vauxhall Ski Slope

With an undulating 200-metre-long steel roof canopy rising up at one end like two steel tuning forks, Vauxhall Bus Station is commonly referred to as Vauxhall Ski Slope.

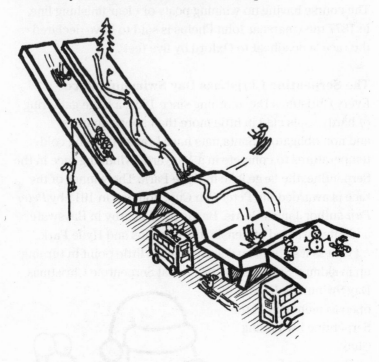

A NIGHT ON THE TOWN

Chapter 15

YOUR ROOM, SIR

In 1892, actress Lillie Langtry moved into 21 Pont Street, near Sloane Square. While there, the house became part of the Cadogan Hotel. Undeterred by the change of ownership, Langtry continued to live in her newly acquired hotel suite until 1897, and it was here that she courted Edward, the future King of England. Langtry's is now a restaurant within the hotel.

Edward and his famed mistress may well have been sharing more than a cream tea in the Cadogan's restaurant when, in 1895, playwright and poet Oscar Wilde was arrested in Room 118, accused of committing acts of gross indecency with 'unknown male persons'. At his later trial, Wilde was found guilty of similar charges – again with 'unknown male persons' – in both Rooms 346 and 362 of the Savoy. The 'unknown male persons' was in fact his lover, Lord Alfred Douglas.

If only he had put out a 'do not disturb' sign…

Savoy Hotel, the Strand

It was September 1953, and two keen American fishermen were staying at the Savoy. Attending a party, discussion turned to the chances of casting a fly from the hotel's roof, over the gardens and Victoria Embankment, into the River Thames. In disagreement, the pair shook hands on a £1,000 wager. A professional fly-fisherman was sought and, early the following month, Lt Col Esmond Drury rose to the challenge. While a policeman stopped the traffic on the busy thoroughfare, Drury, strapped to a pole on the hotel's roof, cast his 2oz fishing lead.

On his first attempt, the lead sailed over the hotel's garden and the four lanes of halted traffic and plopped into the River Thames as planned: a distance later measured at 105 yards (96 metres).

Brown's Hotel, Mayfair

In 1876, Alexander Graham Bell made the first successful telephone call in Britain. He was, at the time, in Brown's Hotel in Dover Street, Mayfair.

During the Second World War, it was from Room 36 of Brown's that the exiled Dutch government – by all accounts, no more than two men and a dog – declared war on Japan.

Claridge's Hotel, Mayfair

King Peter II of Yugoslavia and his wife spent much of the Second World War living in exile in Suite 212 of Claridge's Hotel in Mayfair. On 17 June 1945, Prime Minister Winston Churchill declared the suite Yugoslav territory for the day to allow the royal son to be born on Yugoslav soil. In doing so, the newly born Crown Prince Alexander retained the right to supersede his father as the future King of Yugoslavia.

Great Northern Hotel, King's Cross

The stairwells and corridors of the Great Northern Hotel, adjacent to King's Cross station, are painted with a shade of grey known as 'Elephant's Breath'.

Hotel Russell, Bloomsbury

Built in 1898 by the architect C. Fitzroy Doll, Hotel Russell in Russell Square has a restaurant and ballroom almost identical to another of Doll's grand designs: the dining room of the famed ocean liner, RMS *Titanic*.

Eel Pie Hotel, Eel Pie Island

Originally known as Twickenham Ait, Eel Pie Island – in the River Thames at Twickenham – changed its name on the back of the popularity of the eel pies sold to visitors and passing river trade from what was later to become the Eel Pie Hotel.

Renowned in the fifties for jazz and sex, by the 1960s the hotel was playing regular host to the likes of The Rolling Stones, The Who, Pink Floyd and David Bowie.

Lacking money for renovation work, Eel Pie Hotel closed in 1967. Briefly reopening in 1969 as Colonel Barefoot's Rock Garden, by the following year it had become the UK's largest hippie commune. The hotel eventually burned down in 1971.

Chapter 16

WAITER

The word 'scoff', as in the expression 'to scoff your food', comes from Auguste Escoffier, the first chef of the Savoy Hotel. In 1893, Escoffier created the Pêche Melba, otherwise known as the Peach Melba dessert, in celebration of Australian soprano singer Dame Nellie Melba's visit to London.

From scoffing to quaffing, time to wine and dine...

Frank's Café and Campari Bar
If you're looking to dine with a fresh breeze and fine views across the river to the City, Frank's Café and Campari Bar, situated on the top floor of a Peckham multistorey car park, comes highly recommended; and there's no shortage of parking.

Rules

Opening its doors in 1798, Rules is London's oldest restaurant. The side door immediately to the right of Rules's main entrance is said to have been added for the Prince of Wales (later King Edward VII), so that he could entertain his mistress, actress Lillie Langtry, in a private room above the restaurant. The 'Edward VII' room, along with the 'Charles Dickens' (one can only presume that the revered writer also enjoyed his privacy), have since been opened by the restaurant as a cocktail bar.

The Buck's Club

A mixture of orange juice and champagne, the Buck's Fizz cocktail was first created by barman Malachy McGarry at the Buck's Club, a gentleman's club at 18 Clifford Street, Mayfair.

Limmer's Hotel

Contrary to popular belief that the drink originated in New York, the gin, lemon juice, soda water and sugar-based cocktail John Collins was first created by John Collins, head barman from 1790–1817 at Limmer's Hotel, on the corner of St George's Street and Conduit Street, Mayfair.

In case you think John Collins is a typing error, as the cocktail's formula altered to be made with the sweeter gin Old Tom, the cocktail became known as a Tom Collins.

Sadly, the bar where the John or Tom Collins originated is long past last orders: Limmer's Hotel has now closed.

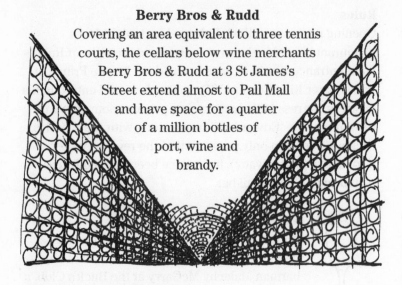

Berry Bros & Rudd
Covering an area equivalent to three tennis
courts, the cellars below wine merchants
Berry Bros & Rudd at 3 St James's
Street extend almost to Pall Mall
and have space for a quarter
of a million bottles of
port, wine and
brandy.

Hindostanee Coffee House

Opening in 1809, the Hindostanee Coffee House at
34 George Street, Marylebone, was the first Indian restaurant
in Britain. Sadly, Britain wasn't yet ready for Indian food,
and the owner, a Deen Mahomet, went bankrupt three years
later. Under new ownership, the Hindostanee carried on,
eventually serving its last plate of pilau rice in 1833.

Peter Jones

Should you require caffeine refreshment, the brasserie in
Peter Jones department store in Sloane Square serves coffee
from beans that have passed through, and been retrieved
from, an Indonesian cat's faeces. Just be aware before
ordering that *kopi luwak*, to give it its proper name, is the
world's most expensive coffee.

If you can't remember *kopi luwak*, just ask for a de-cat
cappuccino.

Zizzi

On 24 April 2007, unnamed Polish r burst into Zizzi Ita restaurant on the Strand, grabbed a l knife from the kitch jumped on a table, dropped his trousers and cut off his penis.

The Cross and Ball

With the originals somewhat worse for wear, in 1820 a replacement cross and golden ball were mounted above the dome of St Paul's Cathedral, 111 metres above the City of London. Once in place, a celebratory meal for 10 people was held inside the two-metre-diameter ball.

CHEERS!

kespeare's Head

was in the Shakespeare's Head pub in Great ssell Street, Covent Garden, in 1762, that the h Earl of Sandwich first asked for a piece of neat between two pieces of bread, thereby giving birth to what is commonly known as the sandwich.

Unfortunately, sandwiches have long since been off the menu, as the Shakespeare's Head burned down in 1808.

Farringdon Station

On 9 January 1863, London heralded the opening of the 'Underground' with a four-mile line carrying steam trains from Paddington to Farringdon.

Having disembarked from the first train, a celebratory banquet for 600 shareholders and special guests was held on the platform at Farringdon, a short distance from its present location.

WAITER!

London's Great Beer Flood

On 17 October 1814, a seven-metre-high vat of beer that had been fermenting for months on the roof of the Horse Shoe Brewery burst its hoops. The explosion – said to have been heard up to five miles away – ruptured other nearby vats and a deluge of more than 1.25 million litres of beer smashed through the building's walls, pouring out into surrounding streets. Eight people were drowned, and the tidal wave of beer destroyed two nearby houses and the wall of the Tavistock Arms pub in Great Russell Street. One man, not wishing the beer to go to waste, later died of alcoholic poisoning.

The Horse Shoe Brewery was demolished in 1922 and the site – on the corner of Oxford Street and Tottenham Court Road – is now the Dominion Theatre.

Clink Restaurant

Between Sutton and Banstead on the southern border of Greater London, High Down Prison is home to the Clink Restaurant. With the food prepared and served by inmates, the restaurant opens for a two-hour leisurely breakfast – plenty of time for the All-Day Full English – but lunch bookings are from 12–12.30 only, so you may wish to skip the soup and not count on a pudding.

The restaurant is also alcohol free and, with plastic knives and forks, don't expect to find anything too tough to cut on the menu.

Arrival time is one hour before booking time to allow for security checks.

If you wish for a little something to take home in remembrance of your visit, the restaurant sells a range of products, including honey from the prison's own beehives…

…And, for the festive season, home-made Christmas puddings.

If you ask nicely, they may even return your mobile phone, along with the set of fingerprints and photo of you taken upon entry.

Chapter 17

IN THE CLUB

Groucho Marx famously once remarked that he wouldn't care to belong to a club that would accept him as a member…

The Flyfishers' Club

> *'Fly fishing may be a very pleasant amusement; but angling or float fishing I can only compare to a stick and a string, with a worm at one end and a fool at the other.'*

> (*Instructions to Young Sportsmen* by Colonel Peter Hawker, 1824)

Founded in 1884 for 'the social intercourse of gentlemen interested in the art of fly fishing', from 1907 until the club's headquarters were destroyed during the Blitz, The Flyfishers' Club spread its tackle in Swallow Street, Piccadilly.

In true British spirit, The Flyfishers' Club rose to cast its vote another day, with members now meeting to recount their fishy tales on the second floor of the Savile Club at 69 Brook Street, Mayfair.

Should a club member return from an unrewarding day by the bank of a murky canal and not be in the mood for social intercourse, the club proudly boasts an extensive library of more than 3,000 works on the subject of fishing, including an almost complete collection of *The Fishing Gazette*; the literary tome *Floating Flies and How to Dress Them* by F. M. Halford; and the classic *The Way of a Trout with a Fly* by G. E. M. Skues.

Although not open to the public, The Flyfishers' Club's museum of fishing memorabilia proudly boasts an extensive collection of fishing rods, rod boxes and fish mounted in glass cabinets, while the collection of historic flies includes a Greenwell's Glory, said to be tied by the great Canon Greenwell himself.

Patronised by none other than Charles, Prince of Wales, sadly The Flyfishers' Club is for gentlemen only; but ladies, do not despair, the club thoughtfully provides a ladies' anteroom, and you are more than welcome for coffee mornings, afternoon tea and a bite to eat in the evening.

Handlebar Club of Great Britain

Founded in 1947, the moustachioed members of the Handlebar Club of Great Britain meet at 8 p.m. on the first Friday of the month at the Windsor Castle pub in Crawford Place, Paddington. Unlike The Flyfishers' Club, membership is open to both men and women.

Eccentric Club (UK)

With the stereotypical image of an eccentric being that of a recluse lost in their own private little world, one would think that a meeting of the Eccentric Club (UK) would be as well attended as the biannual gathering of the Apathy Society. That is perhaps why members of the Eccentric Club (UK), no longer able to afford their own premises, meet in the American Bar of the East India Club in St James's Square.

It may also come as no surprise to find that the club's patron is none other than Prince Philip, the Duke of Edinburgh, and that his son, Prince Charles, the Prince of Wales, has for many years been an honorary life member.

Turf Club

Nothing whatsoever to do with the laying of lawns, the Turf Club is considered by some to be the most exclusive gentlemen's club in London. Founded in 1861, it was at the

Turf Club's original premises in Bennett Street in St James's that the rules of the card game whist were drawn up.

Now residing a mere lawn or two away at 5 Carlton Terrace, the club referred to as 'the bastion of English aristocracy', with both Princes William and Harry as honorary members, lists its activities as 'social, primarily sports and cards'.

Macaroni Club

With a liking for all things Italian – from high fashion to the exotic, continental dish of macaroni – in the mid-eighteenth century a group of young aristocratic men would regularly gather to dine at what became known as the 'macaroni table' at Almack's Assembly Rooms in King Street, St James.

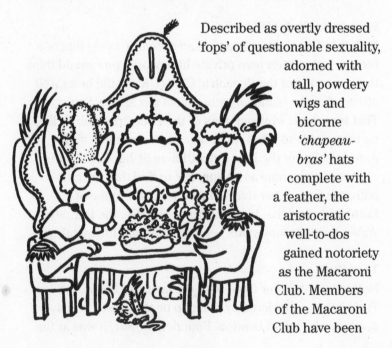

Described as overtly dressed 'fops' of questionable sexuality, adorned with tall, powdery wigs and bicorne *'chapeau-bras'* hats complete with a feather, the aristocratic well-to-dos gained notoriety as the Macaroni Club. Members of the Macaroni Club have been described as a precursor to the 'dandy' and, in its most modern form, the image-conscious metrosexual.

Paying homage to the questionable fashion sense of members of the Macaroni Club, the lyrics to 'Yankee Doodle'...

> *Yankee Doodle went to town*
> *A-riding on a pony;*
> *Stuck a feather in his hat*
> *And called it macaroni.*

...were penned – story tells – by British troops to mock the dishevelled battle dress of their American compatriots during the French and Indian War of 1754–63. Turning the table, the Americans adopted 'Yankee Doodle' as their patriotic song (see 'Lucy Locket', page 175).

The site of Almack's is now an office block, but a plaque marks the spot.

White's

The oldest and most exclusive of gentlemen's clubs, White's maintains a reputation for the outlandish betting behaviour of its members, with all wagers recorded in the club's famed 'betting book'. The book records that in 1939, Tony Milbanke bet fellow member, Richard Sutton, that he could not hit a golf ball from Tower Bridge to the front door of the club in under 200 strokes.

Sutton reached the club in 142 strokes, having taken 40 strokes to get the ball from the gutter to the front door.

The Kennel Club

If you wish to renew your dog licence, the headquarters of the Kennel Club can be found at 1–5 Clarges Street, just north of Piccadilly.

Beefsteak Club

Founded in 1705 for intellectual after-theatre discussion regarding liberty, inter-class mixing and beefsteak, the Beefsteak Club – at times known as the Sublime Society of Beefsteaks – has, by all accounts, met at various locations throughout its long history. To this day, male-only members, dressed in blue coats and buff waistcoats secured with brass buttons that bear the words 'Beef and Liberty', still gather for meetings at 9 Irving Street, just east of Leicester Square. By tradition, members and their guests dine – either here or in a private room at the Boisdale Club and Restaurant in Belgravia – at one long table and, to save the awful inconvenience of having to remember names, the club steward and attendant waiters are, to a man, addressed as 'Charles'.

Legend has it that, in 1926, police raided the Beefsteak Club, mistakenly thinking it to be a brothel. Arresting four men, they found them to be the Governor of the Bank of England, the Chancellor of the Exchequer, the Archbishop of Canterbury and the Prime Minister.

Wolf Club

Fountain Court, a narrow passage off the Strand, was once home to the Fountain Tavern. In the 1820s, Shakespearian actor Edmund Kean founded the Wolf Club in what had by then become The Coal Hole. The club's single membership requirement was that a man's wife would not allow him to sing in the bath; that, and – by all accounts – having a liking for drunken orgies.

By the late nineteenth century The Coal Hole had served its last customer, with Fountain Court redeveloped to become part of the Savoy Buildings. Raking over the warm coals, it wasn't long before a new Coal Hole pub opened nearby, occupying the apparent former coal cellar of the Savoy Hotel. A good few bath-lengths from Fountain Court, the pub's claims of its former bawdy glory are perhaps best viewed through a pair of beer goggles.

Speaking of beer...

Chapter 18

CHEERS!

Now demolished, the Bowl Inn in St Giles High Street, close to Tottenham Court Road Underground station, was where condemned prisoners were allowed a final pint of beer on the journey from Newgate Prison to the former Tyburn Gallows at Marble Arch.

According to folklore, the expression 'one for the road' derives from the drinking of the prisoner's last pint, the 'road' in question being Oxford Street. The executioner – not allowed a drink – would remain outside on the cart – hence the expression 'on the wagon'.

That sobering thought leads us to the tale of a few of London's pubs and inns…

The Dove
The story goes that James Thomson wrote the words to the poem 'Rule, Britannia' – later set to music by Thomas Arne – in The Dove in Upper Mall, Hammersmith.

At 4ft 2 in x 7ft (1.27 x 2.39 metres), The Dove holds the record for London's smallest pub bar, a bar which in its time

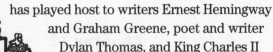

has played host to writers Ernest Hemingway and Graham Greene, poet and writer Dylan Thomas, and King Charles II and his long-time mistress, Nell Gwyn. Or, so say a number of London guidebooks. If King Charles II did visit the pub, he would've needed more than a bar stool to prop him up, as The Dove wasn't built until the latter half of the eighteenth century, at least 60 years after his death.

Carpenter's Arms

One-time owned by famed gangsters Ronnie and Reggie Kray, the Carpenter's Arms pub in Cheshire Street, Spitalfields, is said to have once had a bar made – thanks to the notorious twins – from the lid of a coffin.

Bald Faced Stag

Nestled between Wimbledon Common and Richmond Deer Park, in the seventeenth century Putney Vale was home to the Bald Faced Stag. An infamous drinking den for highwaymen on the road from London to Portsmouth, the

Bald Faced Stag eventually called last orders, remaining closed until – in 1912 – racing driver Kenelm Lee Guinness established a workshop in the basement.

Following successful sales of his high-performance KLG spark plug, Guinness founded the Robin Hood Works, expanding to create a production line in the former pub's outbuildings.

The Robin Hood Works went on to build two world land-speed record-breaking cars: Sir Malcolm Campbell's *Blue Bird* and Major Henry Segrave's *Golden Arrow*. Campbell claimed the record in 1927, reaching almost 175mph on the Pendine Sands of Carmarthen Bay, South Wales. Two years later Segrave broke the record, reaching 231mph at Daytona, Florida.

In 1927, Guinness sold the Robin Hood Works to Smith's Industries and, with the company continuing to expand, the former Bald Faced Stag and outbuildings were replaced with a new building featuring a distinctive large clock.

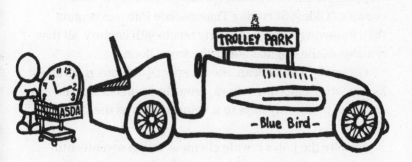

Smith's Industries have long since moved on and the famous landmark clock is now part of an Asda supermarket.

The Anchor

Overlooking the City of London
from the south bank of the
River Thames, it was from the
Anchor Tavern in Bankside
in 1666 that Member of
Parliament and famous diarist
Samuel Pepys wrote of the
spread of the Great
Fire of London.

The historic tavern
features in the 1996 film
Mission: Impossible, where Tom
Cruise's character, Ethan Hunt, is seen relaxing with
a pint on the terrace.

Prospect of Whitby

Dating back to around 1520, the Prospect of Whitby in
Wapping would be a strong contender for the coveted
crown of Oldest Surviving Thames-Side Pub – excepting
that, following a fire in the early nineteenth century, all that
remains of the original pub is the stone floor.

Originally The Pelican, the Prospect's dubious reputation
as a meeting place for sailors, smugglers and cut-throats
gave rise in its early days to it being known as the Devil's
Tavern.

Despite the pub's lowlife clientele, in the seventeenth
century it was frequented by Lord Chief Justice George
Jeffreys, affectionately known as 'The Hanging Judge'.
With the Prospect of Whitby affording excellent views of
Execution Dock (see page 252), the judge would take his
seat to watch proceedings.

The Only Running Footman

It was one thing owning a carriage in seventeenth-century London, but with narrow cobbled streets crowded with animals and people, a footman was needed to run ahead, pay tolls and clear the route. After the Great Fire of 1666, London's streets were rebuilt wider, and the need for footmen gradually died out.

In 1749, with his running days all but over, one of London's last footmen bought a pub at the back of a mews in Berkeley Street, Mayfair. Previously called I Am the Only Running Footman, in the early nineteenth century the name of the pub was shortened to The Only Running Footman.

Fitzroy Tavern

It was in the Fitzroy Tavern, on the corner of Charlotte Street and Windmill Street in the Fitzrovia area of Holborn, that Dylan Thomas would give away poetry written on beer mats to passing women of his fancy. Other former clientele include writer George Orwell, playwright George Bernard Shaw and Coco the Clown.

Since the 1980s, the Fitzroy Tavern has been a regular meeting place for fans of *Doctor Who*. If you fancy an evening discussing daleks in a bar echoing to the sound of 'exterminate' at regular intervals, fans meet on the first Thursday of each month.

Hand and Racquet

Gaining its name from King Charles II's nearby tennis court, the Hand and Racquet pub – on the corner of Whitcomb Street and Orange Street, just south of Leicester Square – used to be the regular haunt of comedians Tony Hancock,

Tommy Cooper and Sid James, and *Steptoe and Son* and *Hancock's Half Hour* writers Ray Galton and Alan Simpson.

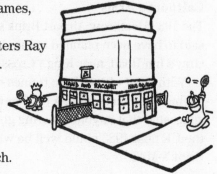

Don't expect service at the bar, as the Hand and Racquet has long since broken serve and called game, set and match.

Blue Anchor

Gustav Holst worked on composing the 'Hammersmith Suite' while frequenting the Blue Anchor pub in Hammersmith. The riverside pub appeared in the end credits of the TV series *Minder* and in the film *Sliding Doors*.

Blue Posts

In the 1925 animated film *The Lost World*, a dinosaur is seen coming down Berwick Street in Soho and poking its head through the upstairs window of the Blue Posts pub. The creature may well have been looking for the vaudeville artist Jessie Matthews, who used to live upstairs.

There are a number of Blue Posts pubs in Soho, one theory being that the posts once marked the boundary of a royal hunting ground, Soho taking its name from 'So Ho!', once used as a cry in rabbit hunting – much like 'Tally Ho!' is called out in fox hunting.

Calthorpe Arms

The 1983 Heathrow Airport Brink's-MAT gold robbery was said to have been planned in the Calthorpe Arms, in the Gray's Inn Road, near King's Cross.

With most of the three tonnes of stolen gold never having been recovered, a BBC news article has since suggested that anyone wearing gold jewellery purchased in the UK post-1983 could well be wearing the stolen gold of Brink's-MAT.

Swan & Edgar

Before reducing the size of the bar to create more seating space and opening an upstairs room, the Swan & Edgar in Linhope Street, Marylebone, was thought to be the smallest pub in London.

Strangely, the floor of the toilet is made up of Scrabble tiles and the bar appears to be resting on around 700 books.

The Eagle

Up and down the City Road
In and out the Eagle
That's the way the money goes
Pop! goes the weasel.

Immortalised in the traditional nursery rhyme *Pop Goes the Weasel*, The Eagle pub in Shepherdess Walk, north of Old Street Underground station, is just off – not surprisingly – the City Road.

The Blind Beggar

Legend has it that after being blinded and left for dead at the Battle of Evesham in 1265, Sir Henry de Montfort took on the life of a beggar. The Blind Beggar pub in the Whitechapel Road – rebuilt in 1894 on the site of a former inn of the same name – is a lasting tribute to the once-noble knight. History, on the other hand, tells us that de Montfort was run in by a sword and died on the spot.

The Blind Beggar is celebrated as the site where the East London Christian Mission – later to be renamed The Salvation Army – started. Founder William Booth is said to have preached his first sermon outside in 1865.

Nowadays, the wide pavement outside the Blind Beggar is given over to the sale of shoes, beds and cheap plastic goods, quite likely – travelling full circle – to find their way to a Salvation Army charity shop in the near future.

On 9 March 1966, The Blind Beggar gained notoriety as the pub where East End gangster Ronnie Kray shot and murdered rival gangster George Cornell as he sat at the bar. Legend has it that 'The Sun Ain't Gonna Shine (Anymore)' by the Walker Brothers was, at the time, playing on the jukebox. Hit by the ricochet of a bullet, the record fittingly stuck on 'anymore…anymore… anymore…'

Queen's Head Inn

John Harvard – later to be first benefactor of Harvard University – was born in 1607 in Borough, south of London Bridge. At the time his father owned the Queen's Head Inn in Queen's Head Yard.

Following his parents' passing, at the age of 28 Harvard inherited the Queen's Head. Not wishing a life as a publican, he soon sold the inn and sailed with his wife to New England, where – settling in Charleston – he became minister of the local church.

Harvard died of tuberculosis a year later, leaving half of the proceeds from the sale of both the Queen's Head and his extensive library to the new college he was helping to establish. The college was named Harvard in his memory.

Having helped finance the construction of Harvard University, the Queen's Head Inn has long since called last orders.

Horse & Dolphin

Built in 1685, in the early nineteenth century the Horse & Dolphin coaching inn in Chinatown was owned by bare-knuckle boxer, Bill 'The Black Terror' Richmond.

Rebuilt in 1890, the Horse & Dolphin – appropriately situated next to Horse and Dolphin yard in Macclesfield Street – is now De Hems café and oyster-house.

The Mayflower

In July 1620, the *Mayflower* sailed from Rotherhithe, on the south bank of the River Thames, on the start of its journey to carry – among a number of other passengers – a small party of religious Puritan Separatists across the Atlantic to begin life in New England.

The *Mayflower* set sail from the landing steps next to a pub in Rotherhithe Street called The Shippe. Since renamed The Mayflower, in recognition of its ties with the 'Pilgrim Fathers', the pub was, until recently, licensed to sell both British and American postage stamps.

Unfortunately, ruining a charming piece of trivia, the new landlord failed to go to the US Embassy to renew the special licence.

Crocker's Folly

With St John's Wood under consideration as the location of a new London rail terminus, hoping to cash in on the resultant trade, in 1898 Frank Crocker invested his money in the building of The Crown, an elaborate, no-expense-spared hotel with stucco walls and ceilings adorned with frolicking cherubs.

With the station built in Marylebone instead, Crocker was almost bankrupted, and The Crown – close to the planned terminus in Aberdeen Place – gained the nickname Crocker's Folly.

Officially renamed in the 1980s, Crocker's Folly has shut its doors for the last time, though its frolicking cherubs can still be admired in the films *Reds*, *The Importance of Being Earnest* and *Georgy Girl*.

Elephant and Castle

Contrary to tales of a Spanish princess referred to as 'La Infanta de Castilla', who was once engaged to King Charles I, the area of south London known as the Elephant and Castle gained its name from the Elephant and Castle Coaching Inn, a public house on a site previously occupied by a blacksmith and cutler. Elephant ivory being used for knife handles, the coat of arms of the Worshipful Company of Cutlers features an elephant with a castle on its back.

The Essex Serpent

One of London's oldest pubs, The Essex Serpent in King Street, Covent Garden, gained its name from an article published in 1669 describing a 'Monstrous Serpent which hath divers times been seen at a Parish called Henham-on-the-Mount within four miles of Saffron Walden'.

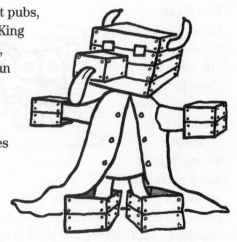

It's thought the dragon may have been made from a canvas-covered wooden frame, operated by a man inside – a practical joke by a local answering to the name of William Winstanley.

Dog and Duck

Built in 1734, the original Dog and Duck pub on the corner of Bateman Street and Frith Street in Soho was a favoured watering hole of both John Constable and Wolfgang Amadeus Mozart.

Replaced in 1897, the current Dog and Duck is where George Orwell enjoyed relaxing after a hard day working for the Ministry of Information at the nearby Senate House.

The Rake

Barely big enough to swing a cat, The Rake lays claim to the title of London's smallest pub.

Despite measuring not much more than  a snooker table, the Borough Market pub takes pride in offering a choice of three real ales, five beers on tap and something approaching 200 bottled beers and ciders.

And if the customers breathe in enough to allow the door to the kitchen to be opened, it also serves food.

The Star Tavern

The Great Train Robbery was planned in the upstairs bar of The Star Tavern in Belgrave Mews West, Belgravia. The robbery, in August 1963, netted £2.6 million, at the time the largest theft in British history.

Then again, other sources suggest that the robbery was planned at the Ship and Blue Ball in Boundary Street, Shoreditch. Some of the stolen money is said to have been hidden behind a false wall in the pub's games room. The pub closed in 1994.

Then again, it appears that it was in The Globe in Bedale Street, Southwark that the Great Train Robbery was planned.

Then again – moving out of London – another story tells that it was at The Globe Inn, a rather quaint pub on the Grand Union Canal at Linslade in Bedfordshire, that the Great Train Robbery was planned. With the train track running along the opposite side of the canal, the robbery itself took place barely the glow of a red signal light away, near the small village of Ledburn.

As the Great Train Robbery gang consisted of 15 rather shady looking underworld characters, you'd think someone might have, at the time, been a little suspicious.

Princess Louise

The Princess Louise pub in High Holborn is noted for its historically listed gent's toilet. It's also considered to have one of the best-preserved Victorian pub interiors in London.

Intrepid Fox

The Intrepid Fox pub on Wardour Street, Soho, gained its name from the eighteenth-century politician, Charles James Fox. A colourful character, it is said that Fox once promised free ale to any person who promised to vote for him. In the 1970s, the Intrepid Fox became a favourite hangout of rock musicians. Legend tells of Rod Stewart not being best pleased when, right under his nose, Mick Jagger attempted to enlist Ronnie Wood into The Rolling Stones; Wood was, at the time, in Stewart's band, the Faces. It's said that the two singers almost exchanged punches.

The Intrepid Fox's colourful days are long gone, but with the name set grandly in stone above an elaborate carving of the pub's namesake on the corner, it cannot be forgotten.

Red Lion

In 1847, Karl Marx and Friedrich Engels held a meeting to discuss their views on communism in the upstairs room of the Red Lion pub in Great Windmill Street, Soho. From

here they wrote the beginnings of what was to be published the following year as *The Communist Manifesto*.

The Red Lion called last orders and closed its doors for the final time in 2006, only to reopen as part of the cocktail bar chain Be At One as B@1 Soho.

Ye Olde Cheshire Cheese

Tucked away on Wine Office Court – a narrow alleyway off Fleet Street – the vaulted cellars of Ye Olde Cheshire Cheese are thought to belong to a thirteenth-century monastery.

Rebuilt shortly after the Great Fire of 1666, the pub claims Mark Twain, Alfred, Lord Tennyson and Sir Arthur Conan Doyle among its former regular clientele. Charles Dickens is also said to have frequented Ye Olde Cheshire Cheese, as did Dr Samuel Johnson.

Ye Olde Dickensian Pub

By the number of London pubs that claim to have been
frequented by Charles Dickens, it's a wonder that the
popular English writer was ever sober enough to pen a
single word, let alone the 750 or so pages of *Nicholas
Nickleby*. As a rule of thumb, if the pub was built after
9 June 1870, the date of Dickens's death, then the claim –
not unlike the traditional English fish-and-chip supper –
is best taken with a pinch of salt.

Spaniards Inn

On the northern edge of Hampstead Heath, the Spaniards
Inn was built around 1585 as a toll-gate inn marking the
boundary to the Bishop of London's estate. In the early
eighteenth century, with his father John as landlord, the
legend goes that highwayman Dick Turpin may well have
found the inn a good place to watch the road for wealthy
travellers on their way to London.

The Spaniards Inn gets a mention in both Charles
Dickens's *The Pickwick Papers* and Bram Stoker's *Dracula*,
and lists among its former literary clients Keats, Shelley and
Lord Byron.

Section 4

GOING UNDERGROUND

Chapter 19

LONDON UNDERGROUND

The story goes that when London's first escalators were introduced at Earl's Court Underground station in 1911, a one-legged man by the name of Bumper Harris was employed to travel on the 'moving stairs' all day to alleviate passengers' fears of the strange contraptions.

Unlike modern escalators, which level off before ending, the top step of the original escalators ended abruptly in a diagonal line, making it easier to step off with the right foot first. For safety and ease of use, passengers were asked to stand to the right, a tradition that has remained ever since.

Time to hop on the down escalator and explore London underground...

Holborn Underground Station Laboratory
Walk along one of the Piccadilly Line platforms at Holborn Underground station and you might notice a small door. Behind this door, a single-person-wide passage leads to a disused platform. Used during the Second World War as

office space, the platform was later converted into a secret underground science laboratory. The laboratory was used by physicist John Barton, one of the founders of particle astrophysics, in an attempt to capture and study deep-level-penetrating cosmic rays.

Developing vacuum tubes able to detect faint light flashes, Barton's 'photomultipliers' were the precursor of modern particle detectors and accelerators such as the much-lauded Large Hadron Collider, currently at work in Switzerland attempting to answer the question of life, the universe and everything.

In the 1980s, Barton moved on to conduct a series of studies on radioisotopes produced in meteorites, which led him in turn to search for 'superheavy elements'. Unfortunately, before he could find them, in 1993 the laboratory closed.

Baker Street Underground Station

Rumour has it that, during the Second World War, members of the Special Operations Executive gained weapons training at a secret firing range beneath Baker Street Underground station. Otherwise known as the 'Ministry of Ungentlemanly Warfare', the SOE was set up to conduct espionage and sabotage in German-occupied Europe.

Woodford Underground Station

Woodford is the only London Underground station not to have at least one letter in common with the word *elephantiasis*.

Greenwich Foot Tunnel

Opened in 1902, Greenwich Foot Tunnel was built to allow workers to get from south of the River Thames to the Millwall docks and shipyards on the Isle of Dogs to the north.

It is said that during the tunnel's official opening, the champagne being drunk by the local dignitaries appeared flat, until the dignitaries took the lift 15 metres to the surface where, due to the difference in atmospheric pressure, the champagne exploded in their stomachs.

Highgate Deep Level Underground Air-Raid Shelter

American TV presenter Jerry Springer was born in 1944 in the deep-level underground air-raid shelter at Highgate.

Leicester Square Underground Station

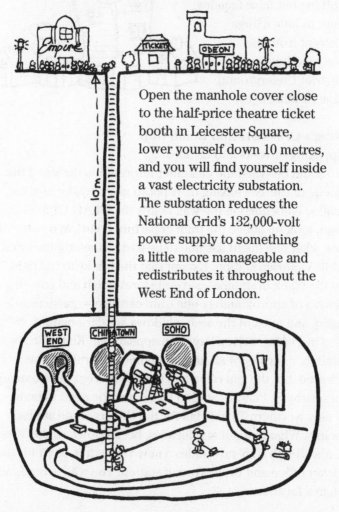

Open the manhole cover close to the half-price theatre ticket booth in Leicester Square, lower yourself down 10 metres, and you will find yourself inside a vast electricity substation. The substation reduces the National Grid's 132,000-volt power supply to something a little more manageable and redistributes it throughout the West End of London.

23 and 24 Leinster Gardens

Disguised as part of a row of grand
Victorian terraced houses,
numbers 23 and 24 Leinster
Gardens in Bayswater are
nothing but false façades,
built to hide a huge
air vent from the
Metropolitan and
District Underground
Line running below.

King's Cross Station Bomb Gap

Speaking of vents and façades…

Stand between the customer information desk and the
queue of tourists having their photo taken by the luggage
trolley embedded in the wall below the 'PLATFORM 9¾'
sign, look up above the train departure board, and you will
see what one might assume to be part of the original brick-
built Victorian station. Except that the bricks to the right
of the black drainpipe – several storeys high and covering a
length of approximately one train carriage – are slightly less
aged, and most of the sash windows are dark behind.

On 11 May 1941, a large gap appeared in King's Cross
station, courtesy of a Luftwaffe bomb. The rubble was
cleared, but the gap remained until the recent development
of nearby St Pancras station facilitated the need to build
a new Northern Ticket Hall for the Underground station
below. What had, for six decades, been known as the 'King's
Cross Bomb Gap' now hides a new ventilation shaft for the
ticket office and Underground station. The wall is little more
than a façade.

Now make your way to platforms 5–8, where cast-iron girders support the massive barrel-vaulted glass roof. You will notice that girders 12–14 (14 being above the large clock) are missing their ornate cast-iron circles, four at the top and three at the bottom. These girders are also new and the wall behind to the left of the platforms is also formerly part of the Bomb Gap.

Hobbs End Underground Station

Most of the action in the 1967 science-fiction horror film *Quatermass and the Pit* takes place on the platform of Hobbs End Underground station. No announcements of 'Mind the gap' here, as Hobbs End was a fictitious station on the Central Line.

Aldwych Underground Station

Standing on the former plot of the Strand Theatre, Aldwych Underground station is said to be haunted by the ghost of an actress, unfulfilled in her dreams of stardom. Had she stayed around, she may well have won a small film part, as the station and tunnels have appeared in countless films, including *Superman IV*, *An American Werewolf in London*, *The Krays* and *Patriot Games*.

Aldwych's success as a movie location comes from its lack of success as an Underground station. A short branch off the Piccadilly Line, the station was used by only 600 passengers a day, and when the cost of lift replacement was deemed too expensive in 1994, the station announcer called 'Mind the gap' for the last time.

Thames Tunnel

From below the Brunel Museum in Rotherhithe, running under the River Thames to Wapping, is the world's first underwater tunnel. At one time described as the Eighth Wonder of the World, Marc Brunel's tunnel was hacked out by men using nothing but short-handled spades, all the time being drenched by sewage-laden water leaking from the River Thames only a few metres above their heads.

Having run out of money, the building of a long spiral ramp at each end for horse-drawn carriages had to be abandoned, and the Thames Tunnel opened in 1843 as a pedestrian-only shopping arcade, with 50,000 people, including Queen Victoria, turning up on the first day to see what was to become the big tourist attraction of the time.

Now part of the Underground's East London Line, on special weekends trains run through Brunel's illuminated 'Eighth Wonder' at slow speed so you can see the shops, still there to this day.

Upminster Bridge Underground Station
When Upminster Bridge Underground station was constructed in 1934, the floor of the ticket office was tiled with a large swastika. A popular decorative pre-war symbol of peace, despite its later Nazi association, the swastika remains to this day.

121 Mortimer Road

In 2008, pensioner William Lyttle was taken to court by Hackney Council after spending 40 years excavating tunnels up to 20 metres in length in all directions under his house at 121 Mortimer Road.

Known locally as the 'Mole Man', having removed an estimated 100 cubic metres of soil, in 2001 Lyttle's digging led to a five-metre hole appearing in the pavement outside his property.

St John's Wood Underground Station

St John's Wood is the only London Underground station not to have at least one letter in common with the word *mackerel*.

Sloane Square Underground Station

The River Westbourne, long-hidden below London's streets, runs through a large conduit above the platforms of Sloane Square Underground station.

Q-Whitehall

According to urban legend, a top-secret tunnel runs from underneath Buckingham Palace, following the route of

The Mall, to the windowless and bomb-proof Admiralty Citadel on the corner of Horse Guards Parade.

From the Admiralty Citadel, a network of spur tunnels – codenamed Q-Whitehall – are thought

to spread north under London's West End, while a further tunnel heads south-east to the Prime Minister's residence at 10 Downing Street.

The entrance to Q-Whitehall is said to be via the windowless fortress on the corner of Horse Guards Road and The Mall, while the large extractor fan visible from the window of the gent's toilet to the left of reception in the Institute of Contemporary Arts building, directly across The Mall from the Citadel, is thought to provide ventilation for the network of tunnels. If you care to investigate, a screwdriver may be required, as the small window, situated in the third cubical from the door, has been covered by a square of painted chipboard.

Given the lavatorial location, this could be considered inconvenient.

Chapter 20

PLANES, TRAINS AND...

At a length of 187 metres and carrying 32 guns, you'd think that HMS *Belfast* would be easy to spot sitting in the middle of the River Thames just upwind of Tower Bridge. To keep the ship hidden from potential spies, it is, however, cleverly painted in Admiralty Disruptive Camouflage Type 25: a light grey with the odd splodge of blue.

Legend tells that – with a range of up to 14 miles (22.5km) – the main guns in both of HMS *Belfast's* forward turrets are currently pointing at London Gateway motorway service station on the M1, 12.5 miles (20km) north of the capital. Were this true, if fired they would blow a very large hole through the middle of the 'Walkie-Scorchie' tower (see page 13). This in turn would solve the problem of the tower's reflected light melting nearby parked cars.

On that bombshell: time to open the bonnet on London's transport tales…

North London Line

Among the frequent passenger services, from Tuesday to
Friday the North London Line runs a scheduled train service
carrying spent nuclear fuel rods from power stations in
the south-east, together with – according to anti-nuclear
campaigners – irradiated waste from Germany
and Switzerland.

Drivers of the trains from the Suffolk power station of
Sizewell often pause for an extended tea break at Willesden
Junction, where they await the nuclear-waste train service
from Dungeness. Linked together, the trains then continue
north to Sellafield reprocessing plant in Cumbria.

Necropolis Line

Departing London's Waterloo train station once a day, from
1854 the Necropolis Line carried the bodies of the recently
departed, along with their grieving relatives, on the 25-mile
journey to Brookwood Cemetery, near to the Surrey town of

Woking. With special funeral trains divided into first, second and third class, one part of the train would be given over to Church of England followers, with the cheap seats set aside for Nonconformists and other riff-raff.

The Necropolis Line also had its own dedicated terminal, originally located between what is now Leake Street and Westminster Bridge Road. The building was later demolished and replaced in 1902 with a new terminal building at 121 Westminster Bridge Road. Eventually, not content with terminating living Londoners, in 1941 the German Luftwaffe terminated the life of the building with a bomb.

Although the Necropolis Line never reopened, the building's entrance still remains.

The Waterpoint
Built in 1872 to supply steam locomotives with water as they entered and departed St Pancras station, in 2001 the Waterpoint building was sliced into three, the top two layers then moved 700 metres north, following the route of the Regent's Canal, to make way for the new Channel Tunnel Rail Link Terminus.

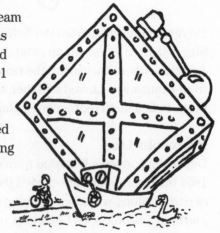

From its new location overlooking the St Pancras Yacht Basin, the brick water tower affords views from inside its 2,400-cubic-foot-capacity cast-iron water tank (complete with original ballcock) of Gasholder No. 8, the gasholder itself having been moved from its previous location. Travelling via Yorkshire for refurbishment, Gasholder No. 8 has been reassembled as a new 'open green space', a place for quiet contemplation within earshot of two of the busiest rail terminals in the capital.

Tower Bridge

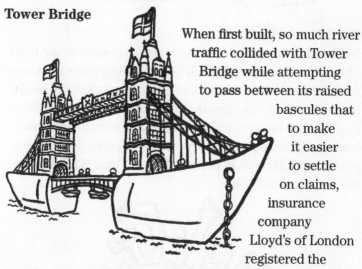

When first built, so much river traffic collided with Tower Bridge while attempting to pass between its raised bascules that to make it easier to settle on claims, insurance company Lloyd's of London registered the bridge on its maritime insurance. And so, on paper, Tower Bridge is a ship. As a ship, the White Ensign – the flag of the British Royal Navy – is flown from the bridge; and as a ship has a bridge, Tower Bridge also has a lookout and command post to control river traffic passing through: all under the command of the captain of the bridge.

And so it could be said that Tower Bridge is the only bridge with a bridge.

Tower Bridge is also the only bridge, quite possibly in the world, to have a chimney. Painted light blue to blend in with the lamp posts, the cast-iron chimney – a flue serving the coal fire in a former Tower of London guardhouse below – can be found on the bridge's northern approach.

Dead Man's Hole

In Victorian London, St Bartholomew's Hospital to the north of the River Thames paid half an old shilling more for a dead body for medical research than Guy's Hospital to the south. As a consequence, before the construction of Tower Bridge in 1894, ferrymen were able to operate a lucrative sideline business by transporting corpses from Horsleydown Steps, south of the Thames in Bermondsey, to Dead Man's Hole on the river's north bank.

The entrance to the 'Waterman's Stairs', just below Tower Bridge, is marked by a plaque.

SS *Great Eastern*

Designed by Isambard Kingdom Brunel, at 692 feet (211 metres) in length and with a capacity to carry 4,000 passengers, the SS *Great Eastern* was the largest steamship to be constructed in the nineteenth century. Unfortunately for Brunel, construction – at Burrells Wharf in Millwall – didn't go to plan. As the River Thames wasn't wide enough to launch such a big ship stern first, and the building of a dry dock too costly, it was decided to construct the *Great Eastern* side-on to the Thames and employ a mechanical slip for the launch. With the construction company falling into financial difficulties, the mechanical slip was abandoned in favour of steam winches and manual capstans.

Watched by an eager crowd of 3,000 ticket-paying onlookers, an initial launch attempt in November 1857 proved unsuccessful. Further attempts employing more hydraulic rams again proved unsuccessful and…

…after more powerful rams were transported from Birmingham…

…the Great Eastern finally slipped into the Thames on 31 January 1858.

Much of the wooden slipway from the launch, close to Masthouse Terrace Pier, is still visible at low tide.

Liberty's

The mock-Tudor rear of Liberty's department store in Great Marlborough Street was built using oak timbers from two decommissioned Royal Navy ships: HMS *Hindustan* and HMS *Howe*.

No. 27 Bus from Teddington to Highgate

Before achieving fame as a singer, Matt Monro was employed as a bus driver on the number 27 bus route from Teddington to Highgate.

In 1966, Monro – by now known as 'the Man with the Golden Voice' – sang the title song of the 1966 film *Born Free*, recounting the real-life story of Joy and George Adamson, a couple who raised Elsa, an orphaned lion cub.

Dagenham Fordite

When the Ford car production plant in Dagenham was facing closure in the 1970s, enterprising workers discovered that the colourfully layered build-up of crystallised paint baked on the car-spraying department walls could be removed and carved into gemstones. The result: Dagenham Fordite, a rare gemstone fashioned from the body-paint of 1970s Ford cars, including the popular Escort and Cortina Mk III.

Chelsea Tractor

Never to be seen ploughing a field, a Chelsea Tractor is a top-of-the-range, four-wheel-drive off-road vehicle, commonly used in an urban environment – typically for the school run.

Stompie

Talking of four-wheel-drive off-road vehicles in an urban environment: walk along Mandela Way in Bermondsey and you will spot, on a piece of waste ground, Stompie, a T-34 ex-Soviet tank. At one time painted bright pink, when not covered in graffiti Stompie usually adopts a black-and-white zebra appearance.

The story tells us that when denied planning permission to develop the small piece of land, local resident Russell Gray reapplied to Southwark Council, requesting permission to place on the land not a building but a tank. Assuming the tank in question to be a metal container of sorts, planning permission was duly granted, whereupon Gray purchased the decommissioned tank – at the time being used on the film shoot of a modern-day version of *Richard III* – christened it Stompie, and lawfully parked it on his piece of land.

Much to Southwark Council's displeasure, the tank has remained in place since 1995, with – according to local lore – the barrel pointing towards their offices.

Free Parking

London streets may not be paved with gold, but they do have an endless number of metal-plate grilles that hold thick glass prisms, set in pavements to allow light into dark cellars below.

Officially classified as private land, it is free to park on these metal grilles, although the owner of the cellar below may not be best pleased.

Chapter 21

TO PEE OR NOT TO PEE

With the introduction of flushing toilets to replace chamber pots, during the mid-nineteenth century the amount of human waste and water flowing into London's 200,000 cesspits increased dramatically. As a result, cesspits often flowed over into the streets, the waste eventually finding its way through a basic open-sewer network into the River Thames.

The summer of 1858 was unusually hot and, with the Thames overflowing with sewage, bacteria thrived, the resultant stench so vile that plans were drawn up to evacuate parts of the city. The year of 1858 in London will be for ever known as the year of 'The Great Stink'.

Talking of which...

Beckton Sewage Treatment Works
Constructed between 1859 and 1865 following 'The Great Stink', London is served by a sewer network that has grown to extend over 13,000 miles.

Sewers north of the River Thames feed into the Northern Outfall Sewer, a giant pipe which worms its way under the

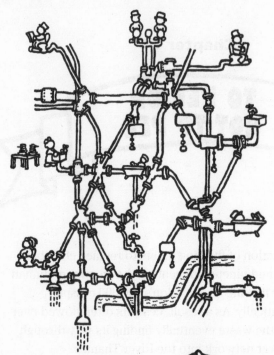

capital to surface at Beckton Sewage Treatment Works, barely the whiff of a warm croissant away from Gallions Reach Shopping Park in east London.

On an average day, the works treats over 100,000 cubic metres of sewage – enough to fill 450 Olympic-sized swimming pools...

...Or enough, every 13 days, to fill Trafalgar Square to the brim of Admiral Lord Nelson's bicorne hat.

Following the treatment process, while the separated clean water is released into the River Thames, a sludge-powered generator compresses the remaining solid waste, turning it into a dry 'cake'. The cake is then burned in giant incinerators to create steam, in turn driving a turbine to generate around seven megawatts of electricity a day.

Currently undergoing a major upgrade and expansion to boost capacity by 60 per cent, Beckton Sewage Treatment Works is set to become both the biggest treatment works in Europe and the third biggest in the world.

Crossness Pumping Station

Designed by engineer Sir Joseph Bazalgette as part of London's sewerage network, Crossness Pumping Station sits on the southern shore of the River Thames at the eastern end of the Southern Outfall Sewer. Anyone who has read the 46 volumes of Nikolaus Pevsner's *The Buildings of England* will know that the respected architectural historian described Crossness as: 'A masterpiece of engineering; a Victorian cathedral of ironwork'.

And a cathedral of ironwork it is:
four giant pumping engines with
flywheels and beams equivalent
to the combined weight of 15
fully grown elephants
housed within the
spectacular ornamental
cast ironwork of the Grade
I listed Beam Engine House,
pumping raw sewage up into a reservoir
that could fill 200 Olympic-sized swimming pools, ready to be
released into the River Thames at high tide.

Crossness Station's engines – gloriously and royally
christened Prince Consort, Victoria, Albert Edward and
Alexandra – sadly pumped their last in 1953, and the
abandoned buildings were left to suffer from vandalism and
decay. For many years on the UK Buildings at Risk Register,
with Heritage Lottery Fund money and the dedicated work
of the Crossness Engine Trust, Crossness Pumping Station
has since been returned to its former working glory.

Leicester Square
Also returned to its former working glory, in June 2010,
Thames Water mounted a two-week operation to remove
an estimated 1,000 tonnes of fat from the blocked sewers
underneath Leicester Square. According
to Danny Brackley, at the time
Thames Water's chief
sewer flusher, the
fat removed was
enough to fill nine
double-decker buses.

Farting Lane

Invented in the late nineteenth century, the Webb Patent Sewer Gas Lamp served to burn off smells from London's vast network of sewers. Methane was collected by small domes in the roof of the sewers, and the gas used to power the continuously lit street lamps above.

A design known as Iron Lilly, the only remaining Webb Patent Sewer Gas Lamp is to be found in Carting Lane, downwind of Charing Cross. Once illuminated by the gaseous product of bowel movements

POOH!

of guests staying next door at the Savoy Hotel, after a lorry reversed into it in the 1950s, the lamp was converted to run on normal gas.

For obvious reasons, Carting Lane became known by the nickname 'Farting Lane'.

Glasshouse Street

Glasshouse Street, just off
Piccadilly, gained its name from
a local 'glass house'
where Venetian
glass was made.

According to
folklore, the saltpetre used
in the glassmaking process was
extracted from the faeces collected
following the bowel movements of
residents of the surrounding houses.

Westminster Abbey

Stand in Westminster Abbey and look down at your feet.
Not only will you see the final resting places of the likes of
Charles Dickens, Geoffrey Chaucer and many great people
of note, but look closely and you will discover that, in small
writing, the manhole covers leading to the sewers below
Westminster Abbey bear the name of the manufacturer,
Thomas Crapper and Sons.

Lion-Head Moorings

London has two lines of tidal defence: the Thames Barrier
and the somewhat older, smaller and lesser-known lion-
head moorings.

Built in the 1860s to cover a very large sewerage pipe,
the Victoria Embankment narrowed the river, thereby
increasing the risk of flooding. Lining the Embankment,
embedded in the pillars below the ornate Victorian lamp
posts, are sculpted lions' heads, each with a mooring-ring

hanging from its mouth. The heads – which have turned a distinctive light green with age – were put in place during the Embankment's construction as an early warning system. If the lions are seen to be drinking, London is said to be in serious and imminent danger of flooding; all Underground stations are to be immediately closed and the city is to be put on red alert.

Always check before buying a travel card.

Great Northern Hotel, King's Cross

The facia of the Great Northern Hotel, adjoining King's Cross station, is curved, as the hotel was built alongside the River Fleet, the river's course following the path of what is now a taxi rank outside of the hotel's entrance.

One of London's 'hidden rivers', long since paved over, the River Fleet is now encased in a culvert and forms part of the capital's sewerage system.

Passing Alley

Legend tells that Passing Alley's former name was somewhat more reflective of its use as an improvised urinal by gentlemen returning home from a night out at the nearby pub. That was until, in the late eighteenth century, the alley's name received a vowel change.

Cloak and Bladder

Following the success of Britain's first public toilet, featured at the Great Exhibition of 1851, public toilets began to appear across the city. Before this, people would simply relieve themselves in the street. For the more well-to-do the city was served by a precursor to the Portaloo: men and women who would patrol the streets, bucket in hand and a voluminous black cape draped around their shoulders. When nature called, the well-to-do would grace the palm of the human portable toilet with a farthing then squat on the bucket, their modesty protected by the black cape.

Arsenal

Talking of bladder, there are more than 900 cubicles and 370 metres of gent's urinals at Arsenal Football Stadium.

Zero Aldwych

On the corner of The Aldwych and Drury Lane, what was once a small underground gent's toilet is now the Cellar Door, an intimate live jazz club with the odd door number Zero Aldwych.

Section 5

LEAFY LONDON

Chapter 22

LONDON-ON-THE-GREEN

Established as the Apothecaries' Garden in 1673, the walled enclosure of the Chelsea Physic Garden contains both the world's northernmost outdoor-growing grapefruit plant and, at nine metres, the tallest olive tree in Britain.

The story goes that, in 1732, seeds from cotton cultivated in the Chelsea Physic Garden were sent to philanthropist James Oglethorpe, founder of the colony of Georgia. Oglethorpe is said to have used the seeds to help establish Georgia's cotton trade.

From cotton to compost, time to relax in some of London's open green spaces...

Primrose Hill

At a towering 78 metres, Primrose Hill affords view across north London and south to the zoo in Regent's Park.

As part of the government's 'Dig for Victory' campaign during the Second World War, German prisoners were employed to dig up Primrose Hill and turn it into allotments.

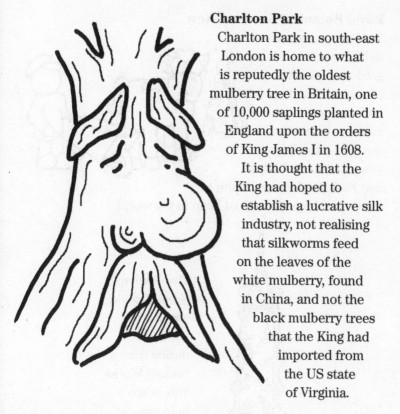

Charlton Park

Charlton Park in south-east London is home to what is reputedly the oldest mulberry tree in Britain, one of 10,000 saplings planted in England upon the orders of King James I in 1608. It is thought that the King had hoped to establish a lucrative silk industry, not realising that silkworms feed on the leaves of the white mulberry, found in China, and not the black mulberry trees that the King had imported from the US state of Virginia.

Phoenix Garden

Tucked away behind the Phoenix Theatre on Charing Cross Road and the Odeon cinema on Shaftesbury Avenue, in the heart of London's busy Theatreland, is a little oasis of tranquillity: the Phoenix Garden. With narrow pathways between long grasses, clusters of bamboo for insects to nest in, and piles of rocks under benches for creatures to make their home, the Phoenix Garden's small pond is thought to be home to the only wild frogs in the West End of London.

Royal Botanical Gardens, Kew

As if the green waste from
the 121 hectares of
gardens was not
enough, add in the
50 tonnes of horse
manure donated
weekly by the Royal
Horse Artillery stables,
and Kew Gardens lays claim to
having the largest compost heap in the world.

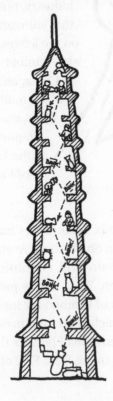

The Gardens'
Great Pagoda
was put to
good use
during the
Second World
War, when a
hole was cut
in the middle
of each of its
10 floors – so
that model
bombs could
be dropped to
test the way
that they fell.

168

Green Park

One of the nine Royal Parks of London, Green Park
was originally swampland used to bury lepers from
St James's leper hospital; the hospital is now the site of
St James's Palace.

Formerly known as Upper St James's Park, a story less
reliable than a bladeless lawnmower tells that Green Park
gained its mono-coloured name after Catherine, the wife of
King Charles II, discovered that her husband had visited the
park to pick flowers for another woman. Seeking revenge,
the Queen ordered that every remaining flower in the park
be removed, and the park be left flowerless. Whether or not
the story has a blade of truth, to this day the park has no
formal flower beds.

Tooting Common

The Oval cricket ground in Kennington was established
in 1845, the turf laid down over what was an eighteenth-
century cabbage patch. The 10,000 squares of turf came
from Tooting Common.

St James's Park

When, in 1905, the go-ahead was given to construct a grand entrance to The Mall from Trafalgar Square, planners came across a problem: every day, for as long as anyone could remember, two women had been bringing their three cows to the exact spot – at the northern tip of St James's Park – where they had set up a stall and proceeded to sell fresh, still-warm milk. They were in the way, and – citing an unwritten right bestowed upon the gatekeepers of the park (from whom they were descended) in the seventeenth century, which allowed them to sell milk from the park's edge – they weren't about to move.

The women found support in both the public and King Edward VII, who himself remembered drinking milk from the stall. Eventually, following a parliamentary debate, it was decided that the women could continue to ply their trade, as long as they moved to a spot further into the park; but only on the proviso that, upon their passing, the ancient right would not pass down to their children.

Admiralty Arch was built, and – with the women long since gone to their graves (and in contravention of Parliament's wishes) – the new location of their stall, bordering the lake north of Duck Island, is now a café called Inn the Park.

Chapter 23

LONDON VILLAGE

Covering around 607 square miles (1,572 sq km) – an area equivalent to around 82,500 football pitches – and with a population edging towards nine million, you can hardly call London a village. Unless, of course, you're an estate agent.

Time to zip up the Aran sweater and share a few pints of real ale with the locals…

Newington Butts

Once a village, Newington Butts is now little more than a short stretch of the A3 south of Elephant and Castle. To add insult to injury, Newington Butts is Cockney rhyming slang for 'guts'.

Highgate

The pub tradition of 'Swearing on the Horns' – the pledging by oath of one's dedication to merriment and debauchery – originated in Highgate village. Commonly seen as a way for local publicans to relieve gullible travellers of their money, after pledging the oath and saluting a set of horns, the financially lightened traveller is bestowed the Freedom of Highgate, thereby gaining the right to kick a pig out of a ditch and kiss the prettiest woman in the pub.

Swearing on the Horns is still practised to this day at both The Wrestlers and Flask pubs, though, due to health and safety regulations, the traditional horns of a live bull have been replaced by a set of horns from an animal of the dead variety.

Dollis Hill

The Colossus Computer, used to great effect at Bletchley Park in Buckinghamshire during the Second World War to crack the German Enigma machine code, was designed and constructed between 1943 and 1944 at the Dollis Hill Post Office Research Station.

The Station has since been converted into Chartwell Court, a development of flats.

Neasden

In 1988, Neasden became home to the UK's first McDonald's drive-through restaurant.

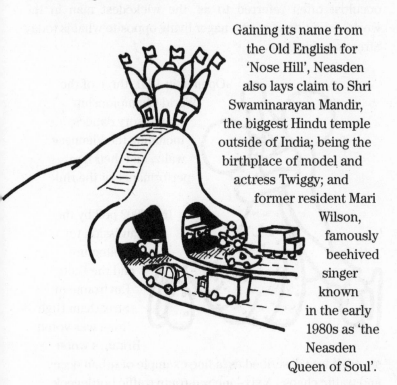

Gaining its name from the Old English for 'Nose Hill', Neasden also lays claim to Shri Swaminarayan Mandir, the biggest Hindu temple outside of India; being the birthplace of model and actress Twiggy; and former resident Mari Wilson, famously beehived singer known in the early 1980s as 'the Neasden Queen of Soul'.

Streatham

Celebrated between the wars as 'the West End of South London', Streatham was the birthplace of London's first Mayor, Ken Livingstone, while other names with local connections include sugar magnate and avid art collector Sir Henry Tate, actor Sir Roger Moore and supermodel Naomi Campbell. Campbell went to Dunraven Comprehensive School in Leigham Court Road.

Before his arrest in 2003, Afghan warlord Zardad Khan lived in Gleneagle Road. Quite possibly outdoing Khan for unpleasantness: born in 1875, Aleister Crowley, famed occultist often referred to as 'the wickedest man in the world', spent time as a teenager living opposite what is today Streatham Ice Rink.

Opened in 1931, three of the World Championship compulsory dances, including the Viennese waltz, had their first performance at the rink.

In a 2002 poll by the Commission for Architecture and the Built Environment, Streatham High Road was voted Britain's worst street; it was described as 'a fine example of urban decay and traffic chaos'. A six-lane red-route traffic bottleneck, every day an endless stream of cars, a couple of bikes and the occasional pedestrian attempt to squeeze their way south down the lengthy High Road in their quest to find the Holy Grail that is suburbia.

Story tells us that in the late 1980s, Prime Minister Margaret Thatcher planned to bulldoze entire streets of Victorian houses parallel to Streatham High Road, dig down and build a six-lane underpass, then fill it back in, thereby moving the traffic bottleneck north to Brixton. Plans were dropped after the Conservative Party themselves dropped Margaret Thatcher as their leader.

In an attempt to make Streatham High Road more pleasing to the eye, in 2009 the local council planted trees along its length. With narrow pavements and a central reservation barely wider than a spade handle, the trees were, rather oddly, flat.

Mortlake
Far from flat, in the 1970s the Stag Brewery in Mortlake was known for brewing the fizzy keg beer, Watneys Red Barrel.

Mayfair
Mayfair gained its name from the annual May Fair, held for two weeks every May at what is today Shepherd Market. The fair was banned in the early eighteenth century due to disturbances.

Shepherd Market today is a charming small square comprising a handful of shops, restaurants, and a couple of pubs. In its day it was – and still is – a renowned and highly exclusive red-light district, the seemingly innocent nursery rhyme 'Lucy Locket' telling the story of a famous prostitute who, in the eighteenth century, used to ply her wares in Shepherd Market.

Also dating from the mid-eighteenth century, the American patriotic song 'Yankee Doodle' shares the same tune as 'Lucy Locket'. But which came first, the kitten or the pony?

Lucy Locket lost her pocket,
Kitty Fisher found it:
Not a penny was there in it,
Only ribbon round it.

Yankee Doodle went to town,
A-riding on a pony;
Stuck a feather in his hat
And called it Macaroni.

Chapter 24

LONDON-ON-SEA

With the River Thames being tidal as it flows through the capital, the riverbanks are classified by Ordnance Survey mapping as part of the British coastline, meaning that London is '-on-Sea'. The coast officially ends several miles inland of London, at Teddington Lock Time to dip our toes into a few of London's watery locations…

Oliver's Island

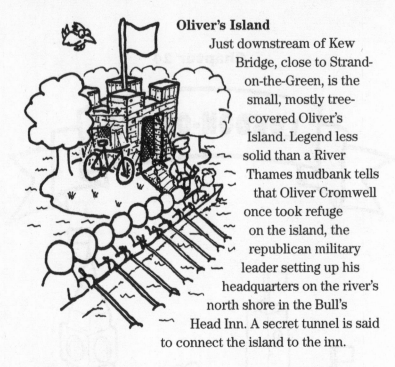

Just downstream of Kew Bridge, close to Strand-on-the-Green, is the small, mostly tree-covered Oliver's Island. Legend less solid than a River Thames mudbank tells that Oliver Cromwell once took refuge on the island, the republican military leader setting up his headquarters on the river's north shore in the Bull's Head Inn. A secret tunnel is said to connect the island to the inn.

In 1777, a river tollbooth was built on Oliver's Island, a wooden structure looking not unlike a small castle.

Flowerpots

The Flowerpots are two small islands in the River Thames, between Richmond Bridge and Richmond Railway Bridge.

Richmond Meridian Line

Greenwich may give the world Greenwich Mean Time and the longitudinal zero-degree Meridian Line, but several miles upstream of Greenwich, as you pass the King's Observatory, Kew, you cross the Richmond Meridian Line.

King George III built the observatory, along with several obelisks, to observe the transit of Venus in 1769. Along the line of the observatory and obelisks runs the old Meridian Line, the observatory setting the official time for London until a standard national time was needed with the arrival of the railways.

Isle of Dogs

No one is quite sure how the Isle of Dogs gained its name: opinion is divided between the land where King Edward III kept his greyhounds and a corruption of Isle of Ducks, so called due to the number of wildfowl that used to inhabit the area, formerly known as Stepney Marsh. What is certain is that the Isle of Dogs gained its unusual name long before it was an island. Bordered on three sides by a meandering bend in the River Thames, the 'island' became separated from the rest of east London by the construction in the nineteenth century of a series of docks, connecting to the Thames by locks both east and west and creating a dividing channel of water across the north of the bend.

Mudchute

Part of the Isle of Dogs,
Mudchute gained its name from
the huge pile of mud deposited
from the chute at the end of a
conveyor belt when Millwall
Dock was being excavated in
the 1860s.

Due to all the rich
Thames silt, the area has
established itself as a
fertile wildlife habitat,
heavily populated
during weekdays by the Canary Wharf
banker in his easily spotted pinstripe suit.

Three Mills Island

Walk away from the North Circular Road across a small
bridge and you are faced with House Mill and Clock Mill, two
striking old mill buildings. This is your first glimpse of the
remaining former working tidal mills on Three Mills Island.

Surrounded by the River Lee
in Bromley-by-Bow, from the
seventeenth century the
three mills were a major
supplier of grain for
London's gin palaces.
They eventually
stopped working
during the Blitz,
when Adolf Hitler
– obviously more

of a white wine and soda connoisseur – attempted to have his Luftwaffe reduce the mills to little more than grain themselves.

Having been destroyed in 1941, the Miller's House was rebuilt with the original façade in 1995, and is now used for educational projects.

King's Cross Lighthouse

On the top of a narrow building on the corner of Gray's Inn Road and Pentonville Road, south-east of King's Cross mainline railway station and three miles inland of the River Thames, sits a lighthouse. Thoughts as to why the Grade II listed folly was built include: a clock tower, a camera obscura and an elaborate advertising feature to promote what was once Netten's Oyster Bar, directly below.

Left to suffer from the elements for a number of decades, the proposed redevelopment of the building has been described as resembling a 'hunchbacked armadillo'.

Trinity Buoy Wharf Lighthouse

Trinity Buoy Wharf lays claim to being London's only remaining true, non-oyster-bar advertising, lighthouse. Originally one of a pair, it was from here that physicist Michael Faraday experimented on his first electrically powered light.

Built in 1864, the lighthouse has long since blown its last bulb, and is currently host to a number of arts projects.

A MATTER OF LIFE AND DEATH

Chapter 25

YOU DON'T HAVE TO BE MAD TO LIVE HERE

Opened in 1851, at its height Colney Hatch Asylum in Friern Barnet was home to 3,500 psychiatric patients. The asylum's most notable resident was serial killer John Duffy.

Closed in 1993, the building has since become Princess Manor Park, a development of exclusive luxury flats, rumoured to be home to a number of celebrities.

Speaking of celebrities...

150 Norman Road
From a bouncing baby until the age of two, footballer David Beckham lived at 150 Norman Road, Leytonstone.

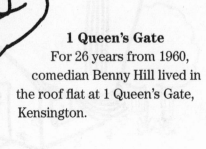

1 Queen's Gate
For 26 years from 1960, comedian Benny Hill lived in the roof flat at 1 Queen's Gate, Kensington.

51 Lower Belgrave Street
Christopher Lee, famed for his role as Count Dracula in many Hammer Horror films, was born at 51 Lower Belgrave Street, Belgravia.

Kingsley Hall
Visiting London in 1931, Mahatma Gandhi stayed in Kingsley Hall in Bromley-by-Bow. According to popular legend, when asked by reporters what he thought of Western civilisation, he replied that he thought it would be a good idea.

51 Barrowgate Road

From 1955 until his death in 1984, much-loved comedian
Tommy Cooper lived at 51 Barrowgate Road, Chiswick.

14 Barton Street

In the 1920s, British
Army officer
T. E. Lawrence –
popularly known
as Lawrence of
Arabia – lived in
the attic room of
14 Barton Street,
Westminster. The
house is now part
of Westminster
School.

2 Hodford Road

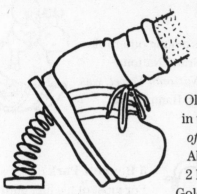

British athlete Harold Abrahams was famously depicted winning the 1924 Olympic 100-metre sprint in the 1981 film, *Chariots of Fire*. From 1923-30, Abrahams lived at 2 Hodford Road, Golders Green.

34 Ennismore Gardens

From 1968 until her death in 1990, Hollywood actress Ava Gardner lived at 34 Ennismore Gardens, Kensington.

15 Dornton Road and 4 Berkeley Place

Fondly remembered for her portrayal of Miss Marple in several Agatha Christie films in the 1960s, Margaret Rutherford was born on 11 May 1892 at 15 Dornton Road, Balham.

From 1895-1920, Rutherford lived at 4 Berkeley Place, Wimbledon.

8 Wildwood Road

Elizabeth Taylor, famous among other roles
for racing her horse to Grand National
victory in the 1944 film *National Velvet*, was
born at 8 Wildwood Road, Hampstead.

5 Bennett Park

For most of his life, until
drawing his last breath
in 1962, 'saucy postcard'
cartoon artist Donald
McGill lived at 5 Bennett
Park, Blackheath.

Taxi!

On 28 March 1921, Derek Jules Gaspard Ulric Niven van den
Bogaerde was born in a taxi in West Hampstead. Adopting
the stage name of Dirk Bogarde, he went on to appear in
more than 70 films.

100 Lambeth Road
Vice Admiral William Bligh,
captain of the mutinous
HMS *Bounty*, lived at 100
Lambeth Road, Lambeth.

Bligh died on 7 December
1817, at 25 Bond Street,
and was buried at
St Mary-at-Lambeth
church.

88 Mile End Road

Seafaring explorer Captain James Cook lived at 88 Mile End Road, Stepney. In 1770, Cook was credited with discovering Australia when he landed at Botany Bay. All that remains of his house is a plaque set into a wall adjacent to a private car park.

32 Parkside

From 1960–72, Formula 1 World Champion racing driver Graham Hill lived at 32 Parkside, Barnet.

4 St James's Square

Nancy Astor, the first woman member of parliament, lived for most of her life at 4 St James's Square, Westminster.

87 Hackford Road

From 1873–74, Vincent van Gogh lived at 87 Hackford Road, Stockwell.

36 Forest Hill Road

Boris Karloff, fondly remembered for his portrayal of
Frankenstein's monster, was born at 36 Forest Hill Road,
East Dulwich.

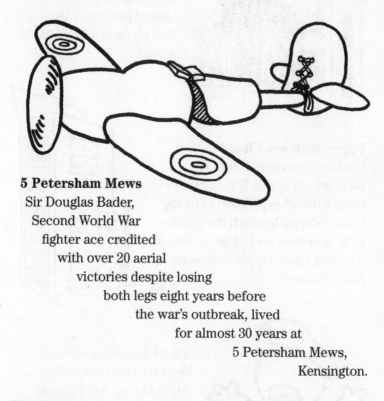

5 Petersham Mews

Sir Douglas Bader,
Second World War
fighter ace credited
with over 20 aerial
victories despite losing
both legs eight years before
the war's outbreak, lived
for almost 30 years at
5 Petersham Mews,
Kensington.

Tite Street

American painter John Singer Sargent lived and worked at
31 Tite Street in Chelsea until, in 1925, his gouache finally
ran out. Fellow artist James McNeill Whistler had earlier
lived barely a brushstroke away, at number 33.

153 Cromwell Road

From 1926–39, master of the suspense thriller Sir Alfred Hitchcock lived at 153 Cromwell Road, Earls Court.

Upper Richmond Road

Captain Lawrence 'Titus' Oates, a member of Captain Robert Scott's ill-fated 1910–12 expedition to be the first explorers to reach the South Pole, was born on 17 March 1880, at 3 Acacia Villas, Upper Richmond Road, Putney.

52–54 Kennington Oval

Field Marshal Bernard Montgomery, 1st Viscount Montgomery of Alamein, was born in 1887 at Oval House, 52–54 Kennington Oval in Kennington.

4 Christchurch Street and 54 Eaton Square

For almost 20 years, Durham Cottage – a small and charming detached house at 4 Christchurch Street, Chelsea – was home to Laurence Olivier and Vivien Leigh.

In 1956 the couple moved to Flat D, 54 Eaton Square in Belgravia, where they remained until their divorce in 1960.

36 Craven Street

Aside from being one of the Founding Fathers of the United States, Benjamin Franklin invented the odometer, swim-fins, the flexible urinary catheter, bifocal spectacles and the lightning conductor. He also liked to take 'air baths'. For up to an hour each day he would open the windows and take in the fresh air from the first floor of his house at 36 Craven Street, near to Trafalgar Square, stark naked.

Chapter 26

INK SPOTS

The Sir John Ritblat Gallery of the British Library has in its possession, among many other pieces of note, the handwritten works of Jane Austen and William Wordsworth, Charlotte Brontë's *Jane Eyre*, Geoffrey Chaucer's *The Canterbury Tales* and Charles Dickens's *Nicholas Nickleby*. The gallery also possesses the diaries of Captain Cook, Lewis Carroll and Captain Robert Falcon Scott, Scott's diary famously recounting the final days before he perished, along with the remainder of his expedition, on the return from their epic journey to the South Pole. A separate room in the gallery is dedicated to a copy of the Magna Carta, one of only four in existence. Sadly, having been partly burned, it would be only marginally less legible if it had been written in invisible ink.

Many writers have dipped their quill into the ink of London. Here are a few of the ink spots...

Middle Temple Hall

Commonly used as a dining and function room for student barristers, writer Robert Louis Stevenson is said to have gained the names for his most famed novel while sitting in the Middle Temple Hall in the City of London.

The hall contains a stained-glass window depicting three deer on an orange background – the family crest of a Josephus Jekyll; and a blue and yellow shield – the family crest of a Roburtus Hyde.

13 Mallord Street

From 1920–39, A. A. Milne lived at 13 Mallord Street, Chelsea. Inspired by his wife Daphne and young son, Christopher Robin, it was here that Milne first created his most endearing children's character, Winnie-the-Pooh.

The Dog and Pot

Atop the reclaimed Victorian lamp post on the corner of Blackfriars Road and Union Street, opposite the entrance to Southwark Underground station, is a wooden sculpture of a dog lapping from a metal pot. The sculpture – a re-creation of a 'Dog and Pot' sign that once hung from an ironmonger's shop on the same corner in the nineteenth century – was put in place in 2013 to celebrate the bicentennial of the birth of Charles Dickens. At the age of 12, Dickens regularly passed the 'Dog and Pot' sign on his way from lodgings in nearby Lant Street to his work at Warren's Boot Blacking Company at 30 Hungerford Steps, close to Embankment Underground station. He referred to the sign in a letter dated 1847.

Recreating a sculpture of a sign Dickens passed on his way to work and later mentioned in a letter could perhaps be considered not the best use of council funds, but then, with neither Warren's Boot Blacking Company nor Dickens's lodgings in Lant Street still in existence, Southwark's bicentennial celebratory options were somewhat limited.

It is, however, popular with pigeons.

354 Lordship Lane

Enid Blyton, author of such children's classics as *Noddy*, *The Famous Five* and *The Secret Seven*, was born on 11 August 1897 above a shop at 352–56 Lordship Lane, East Dulwich.

The flat, at number 354, has since been rebuilt, having been bombed during the Second World War.

Brompton Cemetery

Born at 2 Bolton Gardens in Earls Court, children's writer
Beatrix Potter took inspiration for her illustrated books
from the nearby Brompton Cemetery; the cemetery
contains the gravestones of a Peter Rabbett, Mr Nutkins,
Mr McGregor and Jeremiah Fisher.

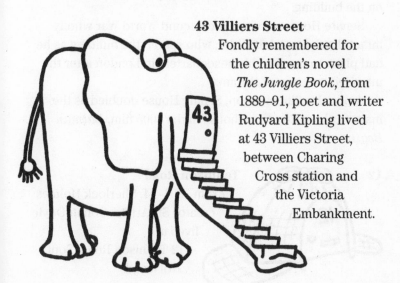

43 Villiers Street

Fondly remembered for
the children's novel
The Jungle Book, from
1889–91, poet and writer
Rudyard Kipling lived
at 43 Villiers Street,
between Charing
Cross station and
the Victoria
Embankment.

Senate House

During the Second
World War, Senate
House in Russell
Square became the
headquarters of a
special department
known as the Ministry
of Information.
Working for the
ministry, writer George
Orwell's hatred of
Senate House led
to him basing the
Ministry of Truth in
Nineteen Eighty-Four
on the building.

Senate House survived the Second World War wholly
intact thanks to Adolf Hitler, who spared the building as he
had plans to use it as his headquarters in London after the
intended invasion of Britain.

A popular film location, Senate House doubled as the
main Gotham City Courthouse in the 2005 film, *Batman
Begins*.

Tennison Road

From 1891–94, Sherlock Holmes
creator Sir Arthur Conan Doyle
lived at
12 Tennison Road, South
Norwood.

Chair G7,
British Museum Reading Room

Karl Marx wrote a great deal of *Das Kapital* in the British Museum Reading Room. The German philosopher and author would sit in Chair G7.

Former Soviet President Mikhail Gorbachev is once said to have remarked that people who didn't like Marxism should hold the British Museum responsible.

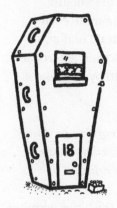

18 St Leonard's Terrace

Dracula author Bram Stoker lived at 18 St Leonard's Terrace, Chelsea, until the lid on his coffin was nailed firmly shut in 1912.

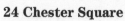

24 Chester Square

From 1846–51, *Frankenstein* author Mary Shelley lived at 24 Chester Square, Victoria.

Chapter 27

MUSICAL NOTES

In the late 1960s, Pink Floyd singer-songwriter Roger Waters shared a flat with his girlfriend, Judy Trim, in Pennard Mansions in the Goldhawk Road. On his commute each day from the Shepherd's Bush flat into central London, just before the Hammersmith and City Line train entered a tunnel outside of Paddington station, graffiti by the side of the track read:

Same thing day after day – have a cup of coffee...go down the station...get on the train...go to work...come home... watch TV...go to bed. Same thing, day after day!

The graffiti inspired Waters to write 'Time', the lyrics warning of how – amid the moribund grind of daily life – time can easily pass you by, with many a person not realising until it's too late. The song was released on Pink Floyd's 1973 album *The Dark Side of the Moon*, the album remaining on the US Billboard charts for a continuous run of 741 weeks.

Time to fritter and waste a few moments on London's musical locations...

Bag O'Nails

On 15 May 1967, Beatle Paul McCartney met future wife
Linda Eastman at a Georgie Fame and the Blue Flames gig
at the Bag O'Nails, a legendary
sixties live-music venue in
Kingly Street, Soho.

At an early gig at the
Bag O'Nails by the then-
unknown Jimi Hendrix
Experience, the
sound volume and
feedback produced
by Hendrix's guitar
performance caused a
number of the audience
to flee the building.

The Cat's Whisker

With barely enough room to swing a cat, the hand jive – a
dance using hand gestures only – was invented in the late
fifties in the basement of The Cat's Whisker coffee-bar-come-
live-music- club, at 1
Kingly Street, Soho.
Closed by the
police in 1958,
The Cat's Whisker
was replaced by the
UK's first Angus Steak
House.

Berwick Street

The photograph on the cover of the Oasis album *(What's the Story) Morning Glory?* was taken in Berwick Street, Soho.

The Roundhouse

With lyrics extolling the virtues of a new racing bike, psychedelic heavy-metal band Hawkwind's hit single 'Silver Machine' was recorded live

on 13 February 1972 at a Greasy Truckers' benefit gig at The Roundhouse, a former railway engine shed in Chalk Farm which had been converted into a music venue.

Chalk Farm Underground Station

Ska band Madness was photographed outside Chalk Farm Underground station for the cover of their 1980 album, *Absolutely*.

Islington Green School

The chorus in Pink Floyd's 'Another Brick in the Wall' was provided by music pupils from Islington Green School, now the City of London Academy in Islington.

29 Melbury Road

In 1974, Jimmy Page, singer-songwriter and guitarist with Led Zeppelin, bought 29 Melbury Road, Holland Park, from actor Richard Harris.

Known as the Tower House, the turreted Gothic pile may well have reminded Page of the band's most celebrated song, 'Stairway to Heaven'.

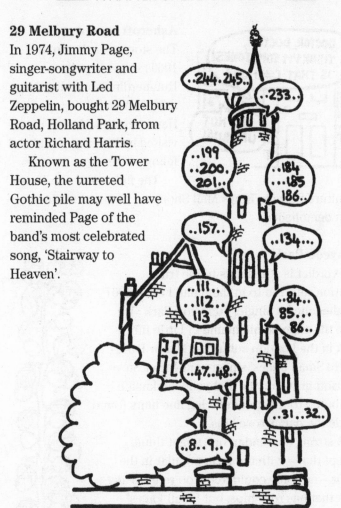

Chislehurst High Street

Reaching number seven in the music singles chart in 1978, Siouxsie and the Banshees' 'Hong Kong Garden' recounts the racist behaviour of skinheads visiting a Chinese takeaway in Chislehurst High Street.

Ashcroft Square

The story goes that in the 1960s singer Engelbert Humperdinck once lived in a flat in Ashcroft Square, Hammersmith. He was often visited by his good friend and fellow singer, Tom Jones.

The flat, above the Times Furniture Store in Kings Mall Shopping Centre, has since been demolished.

Itchycoo Park

The verdict is still out as to the true location referred to in the Small Faces' 1967 psychedelic hit single, 'Itchycoo Park'. We have the claimed nickname of Little Ilford Park in the London suburb of Manor Park, where Small Faces' singer-songwriter Steve Marriott grew up; the 'itchycoo' nickname attributed to the itch-inducing fine hairs found inside the park's rose hips.

A strong contender, one might think, except that – with the term popular in the 1950s – not only could itchycoo refer to any park that has rose hips, but Small Faces' manager Tony Calder claims to have made up this explanation to reverse a BBC ban on the song for its blatant drug references.

But then we have the much larger Valentines Park, barely the sound of a well-plucked guitar string away

in Ilford. 'Itchycoo Park' co-writer and Small Faces bass
guitarist Ronnie Lane cited Valentines Park as the
true location; Lane grew up at 385 Romford Road, near
both parks.

Sadly, Ronnie Lane is no longer with us to argue the case,
but his name lives on in a small street located between the
two parks.

Chelsea Drugstore

When Mick Jagger recounted a visit to the Chelsea
Drugstore in the lyrics of 'You Can't Always Get What You
Want', the building – with its three floors of trendy clothes,
record shops, restaurants and bar – was
a focal point of swinging-sixties London.
The Drugstore also had a chemist, and the
story goes that Jagger used to call in to
collect girlfriend Marianne Faithfull's
prescription drugs when they lived
together in nearby Cheyne Walk.
Unlike the high-street chemists of
today, the Chelsea Drugstore had a late-
night motorcycle delivery service run
by purple-catsuit-clad young girls.
On the corner of Royal Avenue and the King's Road,
the Chelsea Drugstore – where Stanley Kubrick shot the
record-shop scene in the film *A Clockwork Orange* – is now
a McDonald's restaurant.

Hammersmith Palais

Opening in 1919 as the Hammersmith Palais de Danse,
Hammersmith Palais was to be found at 242 Shepherd's
Bush Road, Hammersmith.

During the Second World War, the one-time ballroom dance hall, jazz venue and part-time ice-skating rink was used as a site for building army tanks. Remembered in both Ian Dury and the Blockheads' 'Reasons to Be Cheerful, Part 3' and The Clash single '(White Man) In Hammersmith Palais', the legendary music venue, demolished in May 2012, will not be forgotten.

30 Camden Square

Until her death at the age of 27 in July 2011, Amy Winehouse lived at 30 Camden Square in Camden.

Heddon Street

The cover photograph of David Bowie's album *The Rise and Fall of Ziggy Stardust and the Spiders from Mars* was taken on Heddon Street in Soho.

Lyceum Theatre

The famed live version of Bob Marley and the Wailers' 'No Woman No Cry' was recorded in the summer of 1975 at the Lyceum Theatre in Wellington Street, just north of the Strand.

Finsbury Park Astoria

It was at the Astoria Theatre in Finsbury Park on 31 March 1967 that Jimi Hendrix famously set fire to his Fender Stratocaster guitar.

2 i's

Run by an Australian ex-wrestler known as Dr Death, in the fifties and sixties up-and-coming British music stars such as Cliff Richard, Hank Marvin, Johnny Kidd, Marty Wilde and Joe Brown all played in the basement of the 2 i's Coffee Bar in Soho.

At one time the most famous music venue in the country, the 2 i's pulled the plug on its sound system for the last time in 1970, but the venue – at 59 Old Compton Street – is marked with a plaque celebrating the 'birthplace of British rock 'n' roll and the popular music industry'.

507 Archway Road

Rod Stewart was born on 10 January 1945 at 507 Archway Road, East Finchley, moments after a German V2 rocket had scored a direct hit on the local police station.

Also since reduced to rubble, 507 Archway Road is now an Esso petrol station.

51 Avonmore Road

Later remembered for *Pomp and Circumstance* and the *Enigma Variations*, from 1890–91, Sir Edward Elgar lived at 51 Avonmore Road, West Kensington.

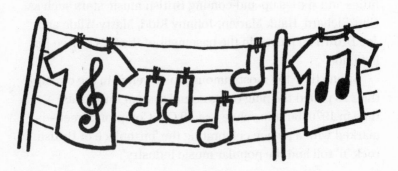

1 Logan Place
Freddie
Mercury,
lead singer of
Queen, lived at
1 Logan Place,
Kensington.

25 Stoke Newington Common
For the first 15 years of his life,
Marc Bolan lived at 25 Stoke
Newington Common in Stoke
Newington. As singer-
songwriter with T. Rex, he
scored his first big hit in
January 1971 with 'Ride a
White Swan'.

306 Vauxhall Bridge Road

The cover photograph of Ian Dury's *New Boots and Panties!!* album, featuring the singer alongside his six-year-old son, Baxter, was taken outside Axfords, a clothes shop at 306 Vauxhall Bridge Road, Victoria.

The album gained its name from the singer's habit of buying second-hand clothes – boots and underwear being the only things that he would ever buy new.

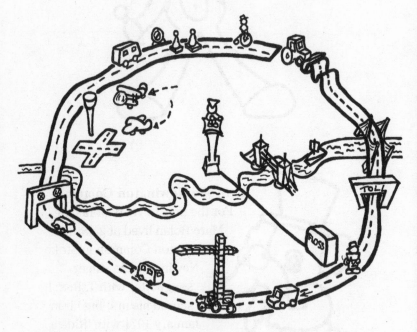

M25

Legend tells that Chris Rea wrote 'The Road to Hell' while sat in a traffic jam on the M25, London's orbital ring road.

Chapter 28

JOHN, PAUL, GEORGE AND RING ROAD

From December 1963 to January 1964, The Beatles
performed a pantomime season of shows at the Finsbury
Park Astoria. Compèred by Rolf Harris and accompanied by
such acts as Billy J. Kramer and the Dakotas, Cilla Black,
the Barron Knights and (who could possibly forget) Tommy
Quickly, over a 16-night period the Fab Four played a total
of 31 shows.

A mixture of comedy, pantomime and pop music, each
performance would begin with the curtains parting to reveal
a cardboard helicopter lowered on to the stage, whereupon
Rolf Harris, dressed as a ticket collector, would climb out,
and all the performers would walk on stage and get a ticket
from him. During the ensuing music, The Beatles would
perform a mixture of comedy sketches (by eye-witness
accounts the word 'comedy' might be overstating the
truth), all of which were drowned out by around 3,000
screaming fans.

Renamed the Rainbow Theatre in 1971, what was
at one time London's top music venue finally closed its

doors in 1982 and, after extensive renovation, is now the headquarters of the Universal Kingdom of the Church of God, a Brazilian Pentecostal church.

Roll up for the mystery tour...

Abbey Road

The Beatles recorded 190 tracks in Studio 2 of Abbey Road Studios in Abbey Road, St John's Wood.

Despite its lack of being a building, the pedestrian crossing outside Abbey Road Studios is officially classified Grade II on English Heritage's *Statutory List of Buildings of Special Architectural or Historic Interest*. The much-photographed crossing famously appears on the cover of the band's *Abbey Road* album.

57 Wimpole Street

John Lennon and Paul McCartney wrote 'I Want to Hold Your Hand', 'And I Love Her' and 'Eleanor Rigby' in a small music room in the front basement of 57 Wimpole Street, Marylebone, the family home of McCartney's girlfriend, Jane

Asher. McCartney lived with the family from 1964–66, and it was on a piano in his small attic bedroom that he composed 'Yesterday'.

At the back of the house, the attic room overlooks Browning Mews. In 1965, during the film-shoot for *Help!*, to avoid the constant gathering of fans outside, McCartney took to climbing out of the attic room window onto a small parapet, then escaping through the top-floor flat of an old ex-army colonel who lived next door at number 56. From here he would take the lift down to the ground floor, pass through the kitchen of the flat at number 10 Browning Mews and exit into the cobbled mews via a small door set between the flat's double garage doors.

57 Green Street
In the autumn of 1963, The Beatles moved into Flat L of 57 Green Street, Mayfair. This was the only time all four of the Beatles lived together.

20 Manchester Square
The photographs of The Beatles looking over the side of a staircase on the covers of *Please Please Me* and the *Red*

and *Blue* albums were all taken inside 20 Manchester Square, the headquarters of EMI Records from 1960–95.

When EMI moved out they took the staircase with them.

Chiswick Park

The promo videos for both 'Paperback Writer' and 'Rain' were filmed in and around the large greenhouse in Chiswick Park. Getting value for money out of the camera crew, The Beatles can also be seen sitting on the low branch of a cedar tree on the sleeve of their *Nowhere Man* EP.

Chelsea Manor Studios

The cover for *Sgt. Pepper's Lonely Hearts Club Band* was photographed at Chelsea Manor Studios in Flood Street, Chelsea.

3 Savile Row

The Beatles played their last ever gig at lunchtime on 30 January 1969 from the roof of their Apple Corps offices at 3 Savile Row, Mayfair. The unannounced live performance later became part of the *Let It Be* documentary.

The City Barge

The City Barge – a Thames riverside pub in Chiswick – features in The Beatles' 1965 film *Help!* The towpath outside features in both *Help!* and *A Hard Day's Night*.

38 Montagu Square

The photograph of John Lennon and Yoko Ono
naked on the cover of their *Two Virgins* album was shot
at 38 Montagu Square, Marylebone. At the time, the ground
floor and basement flat was owned by fellow Beatle, Ringo
Starr. Paul McCartney wrote several of The Beatles' songs in
the flat, including *Eleanor Rigby*.

Chapter 29

TIN PAN ALLEY

The Old Grey Whistle Test was a BBC Two show focusing on serious 'rock' music that ran from 1971 to 1987. The programme gained its name courtesy of Denmark Street, located between Soho and Covent Garden. With its concentration of music publishing companies, by the 1960s Denmark Street had become the place for young up-and-coming musicians and bands to look for their big break and, in the days before the Internet and downloads, to get the break you needed to record a music demo.

The story goes that the musical publishing companies would employ doormen to stand in the reception area of their premises. Men of advancing years, they became known as the 'old greys'. When a band received the first pressing of their demo, the aspiring musicians would play it to the old greys and, if the doormen could remember the tunes and whistle them, the musicians were said to have passed 'the old grey whistle test'.

Denmark Street is known in musical circles as Tin Pan Alley. The name is borrowed from New York, 'Tin Pan Alley' being where many of the offices of musical publishers were to be found in Manhattan. The name is attributed to songwriter and journalist Monroe Rosenfeld, who first used the term in the *New York Herald* in the late nineteenth century to describe the cacophony of sounds emerging from publishers' demo rooms. Rosenfeld is said to have coined the expression after visiting songwriter and music publisher Harry Von Tilzer, describing the piano he was playing – at the time packed with newspaper to dampen the sound – as sounding like a 'tin pan'.

With tin pans in Britain being known as 'frying pans' (the name coming more from its function than the metal it is made of), Denmark Street should really be known as Frying Pan Alley. But then, there is already a Frying Pan Alley near Liverpool Street station...

Number 4: Regent Sounds Studio

With egg cartons lining the walls as soundproofing, it was at Regent Sounds Studio, 4 Denmark Street, that The Rolling Stones recorded one of their early hits, 'Not Fade Away'. The single's label credits music producer Phil Spector as playing the maracas, although – in the days before decimal coinage – it's said he was actually tapping an empty brandy bottle with a half-crown coin.

Number 6

In the days before they acquired punk fame, the Sex Pistols lived in a flat above 6 Denmark Street.

Number 9: Giaconda Café

A sixties mod hang-out, it was in the Giaconda Café at 9 Denmark Street that David Bowie found his first backing musicians, and where he first met rock-and-roll singer Vince Taylor. Taylor later became Bowie's inspiration for his famed Ziggy Stardust persona. Bowie didn't have to travel far as, not being in a position to afford the meagre rent on a flat, he lived outside the café in (reports vary) either a camper van or converted ambulance.

A later hang-out for the likes of the Sex Pistols and The Clash, the Giaconda Café has since been reinvented as the Giaconda Dining Room.

Number 20

With lyrics written over breakfast by Bernie Taupin, fellow housemate Elton John composed the music to 'Your Song' later the same day while sitting on the roof of 20 Denmark Street. He was, at the time, working as an office boy for music publishers Mills Music in the building below.

Chapter 30

A LIFE IN CHEYNES

Chelsea Embankment was built in 1874 to hide a newly constructed giant sewerage pipe, put in place to transport the entire human waste of west London along the north bank of the River Thames, out to Beckton in the east.

Barely a whiff away from the Chelsea Embankment, set back in part from the constant drone of modern-day traffic, over the centuries Cheyne Walk has proved a magnet for celebrities and people of note.

Speaking of notes...

Number 3
From 1969 to 1978, Rolling Stones guitarist Keith Richards lived at 3 Cheyne Walk.

Number 4
In 1880, writer Mary Ann
Evans – more commonly known
by the pen name George Eliot –
lived the last three weeks
of her life at 4 Cheyne Walk.

220

Number 10

Prime Minister David Lloyd George lived, appropriately, at 10 Cheyne Walk.

Number 13

Between 1905 and 1928, composer Ralph Vaughan Williams wrote his first three symphonies, along with the ever-popular 'The Lark Ascending', while living at 13 Cheyne Walk.

Number 41

While living at 41 Cheyne Walk, theoretical physicist James Clerk Maxwell used the iron railings outside to conduct experiments on electro magnetic fields.

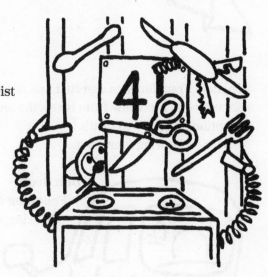

Number 48

From 1968–78, Rolling Stones singer Mick Jagger lived, first with girlfriend Marianne Faithfull and later with his wife Bianca, at 48 Cheyne Walk.

Number 119

In 1851, artist J. M. W. Turner drew his final breath at 119 Cheyne Walk.

Chapter 31

YOU ONLY LIVE ONCE

Benjamin Franklin once asserted that nothing was guaranteed in life; aside from taxes, the only other exception he gave was death.

As the following found out...

Bon Scott

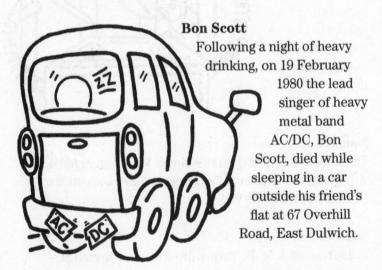

Following a night of heavy drinking, on 19 February 1980 the lead singer of heavy metal band AC/DC, Bon Scott, died while sleeping in a car outside his friend's flat at 67 Overhill Road, East Dulwich.

Jeremy Bentham

At the end of the South Cloisters in the Wilkins Building –
the main building of University College London – stands a
glass-fronted wooden cabinet. In the cabinet sits English
philosopher and social reformer, Jeremy Bentham. As
requested in his will, Bentham's body was pickled and
preserved as what has been termed an 'Auto-icon'.

After being once stolen as part of a prank by rivals King's
College, Bentham's head is now kept under lock and key
in the basement, replaced by a somewhat plastic-looking
wax copy.

Jimi Hendrix

On 18 September 1970, rock legend Jimi Hendrix died of
a drugs overdose in Room 507 of the Samarkand Hotel in
Lansdowne Crescent, Notting Hill.

Judy Garland

On 22 June 1969, *Wizard of Oz* star Judy Garland died of an accidental overdose of sleeping tablets in the bathroom of her home at 4 Cadogan Lane, Chelsea.

Marc Bolan
Two weeks before his 30th birthday, on 16 September 1977, T. Rex singer-songwriter Marc Bolan died when the Mini driven by girlfriend Gloria Jones careered off the road and hit a sycamore tree. The tree, on Queen's Ride, near Barnes Common, has since become a shrine to the glam-rock star.

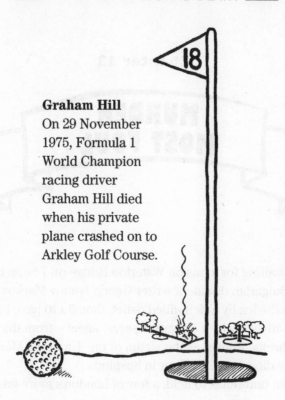

Graham Hill
On 29 November 1975, Formula 1 World Champion racing driver Graham Hill died when his private plane crashed on to Arkley Golf Course.

Mama Cass Elliot and Keith Moon

After performing in concert at the London Palladium, on 29 July 1974, former The Mamas and the Papas singer Mama Cass Elliot died in Flat 12 of 9 Curzon Place, Mayfair. A little over four years later, Keith Moon, drummer with rock band The Who, died in the same room; both were aged only 32. At the time, the flat was owned by fellow singer Harry Nilsson.

Following redevelopment, the former apartment block is now 1 Curzon Square.

Chapter 32

MURDER MOST FOUL

While waiting for a bus on Waterloo Bridge on 7 September 1978, Bulgarian dissident writer Georgi Ivanov Markov was shot in the leg by a ricin-filled pellet, thought to have been fired – allegedly by a Bulgarian secret agent – from the tip of an umbrella. Known as the victim of the 'Umbrella Murder', Markov died four days later in hospital.

From umbrellas to acid, a few of London's more grisly tales...

The Barnes Mystery

In March 1879, a box containing a 'mass of white flesh' was found in the River Thames, having been dropped from Barnes Bridge.

At first believed to be butcher's offcuts, the 'Barnes Mystery' didn't remain a mystery for long as –

after the flesh was found to be human and a dismembered foot was discovered on a Richmond allotment – Irish-born maid Kate Webster was soon arrested, charged with the murder of her employer, 55-year-old Julia Martha Thomas.

Tried at the Old Bailey, it transpired that following an argument Webster had pushed Thomas down the stairs of her Richmond cottage. Fearing she would lose her job, she then proceeded to strangle her, remove her head with a razor, cut her body up with a meat saw and carving knife and boil up the dismembered body parts in a copper laundry vessel. Once 'cooked', Webster then served the tasty 'pig's lard' meal to a number of local boys, who, not realising they were consuming the evidence of a murder, happily ate two bowls each.

In July 1879, Kate Webster was hanged for her crime at Wandsworth Prison; the head of Julia Martha Thomas was never found.

That was until October 2010, when workmen excavating the former Hole in the Wall pub in the Richmond garden of natural history presenter Sir David Attenborough, came across a skull. Tests, including carbon dating, showed it to be that of Mrs Thomas, who had lived two doors away.

Bleeding Heart Yard

According to folklore,
Bleeding Heart Yard –
a cobbled courtyard
in Farringdon –
gained its name
from the murder
in 1626 of Lady
Elizabeth Hatton.
Charles Dickens in

his novel *Little Dorrit* referred to her body being found with
limbs torn apart and blood still pumping from her heart.

It's a pity to spoil a good tale, but in reality Bleeding
Heart Yard gained its name from a sign showing the heart
of the Virgin Mary pierced by five swords. The sign hung
outside the Bleeding Heart pub round the corner in what is
now Greville Street.

79 Gloucester Road

Not long after being released from serving a prison sentence
for fraud, John George Haigh bumped into his former
employer, William McSwan, at the Goat Tavern in Kensington
High Street. On 6 September 1944, Haigh lured McSwan into

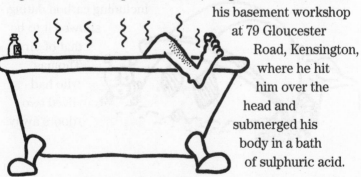

his basement workshop
at 79 Gloucester
Road, Kensington,
where he hit
him over the
head and
submerged his
body in a bath
of sulphuric acid.

Returning two days later, he poured the liquefied remains of McSwan's body down a drain in the back yard.

After McSwan's wealthy parents became concerned about their son's whereabouts, Haigh lured them to the same basement, where they met a similar fate. He then went on to forge the McSwans' signatures, transferring the deeds to both of their properties and a large sum of cash into his name.

Selling the properties and moving from London, Haigh went on to murder a further three victims in a similar fashion, before suspicion was aroused and he was finally arrested.

Commonly known as the Acid Bath Murderer, in court Haigh entered a plea of insanity, claiming that he had drunk his victims' blood before dissolving them in acid. He was found guilty of a total of six murders, three fewer than he had claimed, and hanged at Wandsworth Prison in 1949.

195 Melrose Avenue and 23 Cranley Gardens

In the late 1970s and early 1980s, Dennis Nilsen committed 12 murders while living at 195 Melrose Avenue in Cricklewood. Using skills learned as a cook in the army, Nilsen butchered the bodies, burning the remains in the back garden.

Moving from Melrose Avenue, Nilsen killed another three men in his attic flat at 23 Cranley Gardens in Muswell Hill. Police were called when human remains were found blocking the flats' sewers.

39 Hilldrop Crescent

On 31 January 1910, Dr Hawley Harvey Crippen murdered his wife, Cora, in their home at 39 Hilldrop Crescent in Holloway, burning her arms, legs and various other bones in the kitchen stove and dissolving her organs in acid in the bathtub. Police later found what remained of her torso buried under the cellar floor.

Attempting to flee to Canada, Crippen was arrested on the SS *Montrose* as it entered the St Lawrence River, the first criminal to be caught with the aid of wireless communication.

The house in Hilldrop Crescent was later destroyed by a bomb in the Second World War; it has since been replaced by a block of flats.

10 Rillington Place

In October 1948, Timothy Evans's wife, Beryl, gave birth to a baby daughter, Geraldine, in the top-floor flat of 10 Rillington Place. One year later, Beryl and Geraldine were dead, their bodies discovered by police in an outside wash house. Both had been strangled. Having confessed under police interrogation, Timothy Evans was subsequently convicted of the murder of his daughter, and – on 9 March 1950 – hanged at Pentonville Prison. A key witness for the prosecution was John Christie, who lived with his wife, Ethel, on the ground floor of the same house.

At the time of Evans's arrest, a police search of the small garden at 10 Rillington Place had failed to spot the bodies of a further two women, hidden in shallow graves, along with a human thigh bone, used to prop up a piece of trellis.

In March 1953, John Christie moved out of 10 Rillington Place, leaving behind – along with the two bodies in the garden that the police had missed during their earlier investigations – the bodies of a further three women hidden behind a false wall in the kitchen, together with the body of his wife, hidden beneath the front-room floorboards. All had been strangled.

Eleven days later, on 31 March, Christie was arrested outside the Star and Garter pub in Putney. Having been a key witness at Evans's earlier trial, doubt was put on the conviction. It is thought that Evans's confession, which he later retracted, may well have been fabricated by the police and, although Christie never actually admitted murdering Evans's daughter, Timothy Evans subsequently received a posthumous pardon.

Christie did, however, admit the murder of Timothy Evans' wife, along with his own wife and five other women. One of Britain's most notorious serial killers, on 15 July 1953, he too was hanged at Pentonville Prison.

Just as Windscale was renamed Sellafield to make local residents feel better about an unfortunate nuclear fuel spillage, Rillington Place was later renamed Ruston Close. Located in the Ladbroke Grove part of Notting Hill, the street was demolished in the 1970s to make way for the Westway overpass. Later redeveloped as Bartle Road, the site of 10 Rillington Place is now a small garden.

46 Lower Belgrave Street

Having apparently mistaken her for his wife, on 7 November 1974 Lord Lucan allegedly murdered his 29-year-old nanny in the basement kitchen of 46 Lower Belgrave Street, Belgravia. Lucan fled the scene and was never caught.

186 Fleet Street

Fiction tells of Sweeney Todd, the Demon Barber of Fleet Street, who slit the throats of his clients before dispensing with them through a trapdoor, later to be made into meat pies by pie-shop owning accomplice, Margery Lovett. Todd was said to have robbed and murdered more than 150 customers.

The tale of Sweeney Todd first appeared in 1846 in the 18-part 'penny-dreadful' *The String of Pearls: A Romance*, with the demon barber's shop located at 186 Fleet Street, alongside Hen and Chicken Court. Lovett's Pie Shop was said to be in nearby Bell Yard, a tunnel running under St Dunstan's Church connecting the two properties.

With little on Bell Yard suggesting that it may have once been a pie shop, unless Mrs Lovett plied her tasty wares from a Victorian version of the classic K6 telephone box at the southern end of the street, the story of the Demon Barber of Fleet Street could be described as somewhat overbaked.

Chapter 33

GRAVE MATTERS

With London's expanding population, by the nineteenth century inner-city church graveyards were unable to cope with the growing number of burials. A plan was put in place to build a ring of seven great cemeteries around the capital. Opening for business in 1839, the most famous of these 'Magnificent Seven' cemeteries is at Highgate.

Many a person will tell you that Highgate Cemetery's most famed 'resident' is Karl Marx. They may not tell you that, before rock stardom, Rod Stewart had a summer job there marking out plots in preparation for the gravedigger.

Talking of grave matters...

Elmers End Cemetery
Thomas Crapper, inventor of the floating ballcock and manufacturer of toilets, is buried in Elmers End Cemetery.

After having been finally bowled out in 1915 at the age of 67, cricketing legend W. G. Grace is buried barely a well-struck half volley away.

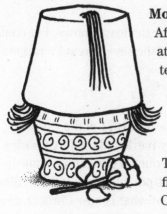

Mortlake Crematorium
After suffering a fatal heart attack on stage during a television broadcast of *Live From Her Majesty's Theatre*, revered comedian and famed fez-wearing magician Tommy Cooper made the final journey to Mortlake Crematorium.

Nunhead Cemetery
Consecrated in 1840, Nunhead Cemetery's short list of celebrity graves lays claim to little more than Charles Abbott, a 101-year-old Ipswich grocer and Charterhouse Brother, and Frederick Abel, co-inventor of cordite.

Pushing up the daisies they certainly are, as the abundance of trees and overgrown vines in the rich soil has led to the unearthing of many of the ancient tombstones.

During the Blitz, the Luftwaffe, determined to create more space for the recently deceased, managed to destroy the Dissenters' Chapel. Three decades later and the Gothic Grade II listed Anglican chapel lost its roof, courtesy of an arson attack.

Nunhead Cemetery may be the least known, but could well be the most attractive of the seven great Victorian cemeteries of London.

St Andrew's Church

Famous for the attempted theft in 1671 of the Crown Jewels, after being dubiously pardoned by King Charles II, Colonel Thomas Blood lived out his days at his home in Bowling Alley, Westminster. Upon his death in 1680, Blood was buried in the graveyard of what is now Christchurch Gardens, near St James's Park. With it later suspected that he may have faked his own death to avoid settling debts, Blood's body was exhumed, and is now said to rest in the graveyard of St Andrew's Church in Hornchurch.

Allegedly, the grave lies close to the church building nearest to the main road, and is unmarked, except, that is, for a faded skull and crossbones.

And on that note...

Cross Bones Graveyard

For tonight in Hell, they are tolling the bell
For the Whore that lay at The Tabard.
And well we know how the carrion crow
Doth feast in our Cross Bones Graveyard.

'John Crow's Riddle' from *The Southwark Mysteries*
by John Constable, 1999

Opposite the Boot and Flogger wine bar and restaurant in Redcross Way – a quiet backstreet in The Borough – a huge pair of rusted iron gates covered top to toe with ribbons, flowers and messages hides a bronze plaque bearing the epitaph: 'R.I.P. The Outcast Dead'. For behind the locked gates and the London Underground hoardings, the derelict land was once Cross Bones Graveyard, an unconsecrated burial site for prostitutes, and later, paupers, until its closure in 1853 on public-health grounds. These 'grounds' were – as excavation work in the 1990s for the Jubilee Line extension revealed – that there were an estimated 15,000 bodies buried in a plot of land barely big enough to house a small funfair.

I say that as – with the sale of the land for development in 1883 declared illegal the following year under the Disused Burial Grounds Act – the former Cross Bones Graveyard was later used for a short time to house a funfair.

The 'shrine' to those buried within the disused graveyard
is maintained by the Friends of Cross Bones, who hold a
candlelit vigil on the evening of the 23rd of each month in
the hope of securing a permanent memorial garden.

East Finchley Cemetery

Comic artist and illustrator William Heath Robinson was
born on 31 May 1872, at 25 Ennis Road, Stroud Green.
Known for his drawings of implausible contraptions,
unnecessarily complex and often involving string-and-pulley
systems, the term 'Heath Robinson' is commonly used
to describe temporary fixes using little more than a deep
breath and crossed fingers.

He died in September 1944 and is buried in East Finchley
Cemetery.

Sir Samuel Morland, inventor of the megaphone, is buried in the graveyard of St Paul's church in Hammersmith

South London Crematorium

The ashes of actor Wilfrid Brambell – fondly remembered as Albert Steptoe in the TV sitcom *Steptoe and Son* – were scattered beneath Tree 3 at the South London Crematorium, Streatham Vale.

West Norwood Cemetery

With its Gothic Revival architecture and 66 Grade II listed buildings, including catacombs, mausoleums and monuments, West Norwood Cemetery is one of the seven great Victorian cemeteries of London. Its most celebrated residents include Sir Henry Doulton, appropriately resting in a mausoleum constructed of brick and red tiles from his own Doulton pottery factory; cookery writer Isabella Beeton, remembered for *Mrs Beeton's Book of Household Management*; and Sir Henry Tate, one half of the sugar manufacturers Tate & Lyle and benefactor of the Tate Art Gallery. Unfortunately, since opening for business in 1837, the cemetery has suffered a two-pronged attack: during the Blitz, German bombers, not content with uprooting people on the ground, uprooted several who were already buried.

And to add insult to injury, since compulsorily purchasing the cemetery in 1966, Lambeth Council controversially dug up between 5,000 and 10,000 of the monuments the bombers missed and reopened the grounds for new business.

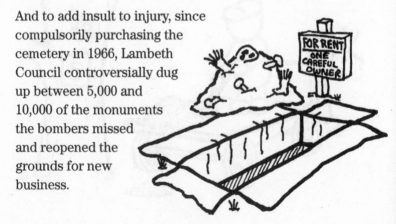

Chapter 34

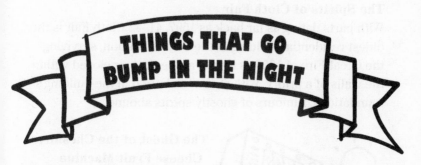

THINGS THAT GO BUMP IN THE NIGHT

Described in Victorian times as London's most haunted house, 50 Berkeley Square in Mayfair has witnessed enough mysterious deaths and ghostly sightings to send a shiver down the spine of even the hardiest of London ghost tour operators. Spooky stories abound, with talk of the spirit of a Mr Myers, who became a miserable hermit after his fiancée abandoned him on his wedding day. Is this the ghostly spectre seen casting its light from the top floor of 50 Berkeley Square in the middle of the night, or could it be the ghost of a Mr Du Pre's lunatic brother: the brother he locked away in the attic and fed through a small hole in the door?

From a miserable hermit to a phantom bus: time to send a shiver down London's ghostly spine...

The Ghostly Bear of Cheyne Walk

Since the late nineteenth century, regular sightings of a ghostly bear have been reported in the gardens of Cheyne Walk, Chelsea. The ghost is thought

to be that of one of the bears killed from the grisly sport of bear-baiting carried out there three centuries earlier.

The Spirits of Cloth Fair

With parts dating as far back as 1597, 41–42 Cloth Fair is the oldest residential building in the City of London, surviving the Great Fire of 1666 as it was, at the time, enclosed within the walls of a priory. With skeletons buried in the building's foundations, rumours of ghostly spirits abound.

The Ghost of the Cheshire Cheese Fruit Machine

The Cheshire Cheese pub in Little Essex Street, just south of the Strand, is said to be haunted by a ghost that has a habit of moving the fruit machine.

Scratching Fanny of Cock Lane

London's most famous ghost story begins in Norfolk, with the tale of William Kent. The year was 1760 and, with his wife Elizabeth having died in childbirth, Kent began a relationship with her sister, Fanny. Unable to marry due to canon law, Kent eloped with Fanny to London, where they found lodgings at the home of a Richard Parsons at 33 Cock Lane, close to Smithfield Market.

Having first loaned Parsons a large sum of money, Kent was soon to go away on business. While he was away, Fanny, not wishing to sleep alone, took to sharing her bed with Parson's 11-year-old daughter, Elizabeth. But all was not restful, as Fanny began to hear ghostly scratching sounds at night.

Kent returned to find his mistress distraught and, fearing that 33 Cock Lane was haunted, the couple moved out. Sadly, Fanny was soon to die of smallpox. With his mistress dead and Parsons refusing to settle the earlier outstanding loan, Kent sought legal action. In return, Parsons claimed that the scratching noises were the ghost of Fanny's dead sister, Elizabeth, telling that Kent had poisoned Fanny with arsenic.

News spread of the vengeful ghost, and Londoners flocked to the house in Cock Lane to hear the eerie scratching and knocking noises. While they did so, Parsons, having charged each a small entrance fee, would interpret the murderous accusations of the ghostly Elizabeth, heard through his daughter.

All was well until daughter Elizabeth was seen to hide a small wooden block under her stays, and her dress was lifted to reveal the source of the scratching – the eighteenth-century equivalent of sandpaper strapped to her inner legs. With the hoax exposed, Parsons was imprisoned for two years. Nevertheless, the interest in 'Scratching Fanny of Cock Lane' has lived on, and has since entered into folklore.

The Spirit of Christchurch Greyfriars Garden

Within listening distance of a Sunday choir service from St Paul's Cathedral hides a sheltered rose garden, enclosed inside the remaining walls of the derelict Christchurch Greyfriars. Built between 1306 and 1348, the original church was part of a Franciscan monastery; it was the Franciscans' wearing of grey habits that gained them the nickname 'Greyfriars'.

With the first Church of Greyfriars destroyed in the Great Fire of 1666, a new church, designed by Sir Christopher Wren, was completed in 1704. Sadly, all but the west tower was destroyed during the Blitz.

Following the floor plan of Wren's church, in 1989 Christchurch Greyfriars garden was laid out as a public garden and memorial. The garden is thought to be troubled by the spirit of Queen Isabella, wife to King Edward II, who was buried within the grounds of the original church in 1358. Their marriage on the rocks, after being sent to her native France to negotiate peace in 1325, Queen Isabella returned with an army and deposed her husband.

The King was imprisoned and allegedly murdered, on the orders of his wife, courtesy of a red-hot poker inserted up his rectum.

The entrance to Christchurch Greyfriars Garden can be found off King Edward Street, as can the side street, Queen Isabella Way.

244

The Ghostly Clown of the Theatre Royal

Credited as being the father of the modern-day clown, Joseph Grimaldi appeared regularly on stage at the Theatre Royal, Drury Lane. Crippled by ill health brought on by his energetic stage act, Grimaldi died in 1837, and it is said that his ghost, still wearing the white-faced clown make-up that he made famous, has often been seen at the theatre.

The Ghost Chicken of Pond Square

One morning in Pond Square, Highgate, in 1626, the appropriately named Sir Francis Bacon put his theory that refrigeration might be used as a way of preserving meat to the test, by plucking and stuffing a dead chicken with snow. A bitterly cold day, as a result of his experiment, Bacon caught pneumonia and died soon afterwards.

Since Bacon's death there have been numerous reported sightings of a ghostly chicken.

The Haunting of Covent Garden

The distance between Covent Garden and Leicester Square Underground stations is 251 metres, barely the length of three Underground trains. If you don't care for the short walk then beware, as Covent Garden Underground station is said to be haunted by William Terriss, owner of the Adelphi Theatre, murdered in 1897 as he entered the theatre's back door in nearby Maiden Lane.

The Phantom Ladbroke Grove Bus
London lore tells of a phantom red double-decker bus, often seen in Ladbroke Grove.

With no passengers or crew, the bus was usually spotted, early in the morning, speeding around the blind bend at the junction of St Mark's Road and Cambridge Gardens. An accident black spot, the junction was straightened in the 1930s, and the ghostly bus has appeared no more.

Chapter 35

LAW AND DISORDER

Before 1823, if a murder suspect committed suicide before they could be tried and executed, they would instead be belatedly punished by way of a stake driven through the heart, followed by burial at a crossroads close to where they had committed their crime.

Found hanged in his cell, one of the last persons to be dispensed of in London in such a manner was a John Williams, in December 1811. His body was buried outside the Crown and Dolphin pub, at the junction of Cable Street and Cannon Street Road, Whitechapel. The story goes that, following its discovery when gas piping was being laid in the 1960s, Williams's skull was displayed for many years inside the pub. The Crown and Dolphin closed in 2002.

On that grave note, law abiding or otherwise, it's time to delve into London's underbelly...

32 Ambleside Avenue

Noted in court as 'the biggest disorderly house in history', it was at 32 Ambleside Avenue in Streatham in the seventies and eighties that vicars, MPs, judges and the like allegedly exchanged luncheon vouchers for food, drink and the services of a prostitute: a meal-deal that surpassed even an all-day breakfast at a greasy-spoon café.

Run by Cynthia Payne – otherwise known as 'Madam Cyn' – the comings and goings of the famed brothel hit the big screen in the 1987 film *Personal Services*, along with the film *Wish You Were Here*, a loose portrayal of Cynthia Payne as a teenager. Meanwhile, Madam Cyn herself went on to seek a place in Parliament as leader of the Payne and Pleasure Party.

Sadly, she failed to get elected.

Cock Lane
In medieval times, Cock Lane – a short alleyway by Smithfield Market – was the only street in London that allowed legalised brothels. How the street got its name is perhaps best left to the imagination.

Silver Cross
Under a privilege granted by King Charles I, the Silver Cross pub in Whitehall is the UK's only remaining legalised brothel.

Serious Crime Directorate 9: Human Exploitation and Organised Crime Command

Set up in 1932 to deal with prostitution and other aspects of London's grubby underbelly, in 2010 the Vice Squad changed its name to the Serious Crime Directorate 9: Human Exploitation and Organised Crime Command.

> SERIOUS CRIME DIRECTORATE 9: HUMAN EXPLOITATION AND ORGANISED CRIME COMMAND – YOU'RE NICKED!

Cheapside

Being granted the Freedom of the City of London is commonly said to give one the right to drive geese down Cheapside without incurring a toll, usually payable to the City of London.

249

Tower Bridge

Aside from driving geese down Cheapside, being granted
the Freedom of the City of London gives one the right to
enter the city with a live animal, for the purpose of making
a sale, without incurring a toll. The right is commonly
misquoted as allowing a freeman to drive a herd of sheep
across Tower Bridge.

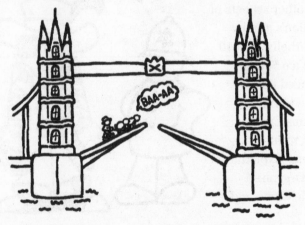

In 1999, freeman Jeff Smith exercised what he considered
to be his right, entering the city across Tower Bridge, albeit
with a herd of only two sheep.

Houses of Parliament

Under an ancient law passed in 1313,
and still in force to this day, MPs
are not allowed to wear a suit of
armour in Parliament. They are
also, according to some sources,
not allowed to die (at least, not
in Parliament).

Technically, on 11 May 1812, Prime

Minister Spencer Perceval broke the law, when he was shot dead in the House of Commons lobby. The only British prime minister to be assassinated, he is buried at St Luke's Church, Charlton.

Cows

The Metropolitan Streets Act of 1867 prohibits the driving or conducting of any cattle through any street between the hours of 10 a.m. and 7 p.m. Contravention of this law, yet to be repealed, carries a maximum fine of £25 per head of cattle.

Pelicans

Unless written permission is granted, it is illegal to touch a pelican in a Royal Park.

Taxi!

It is illegal for a taxi driver, within the bounds of the City of London, to carry either a dead person or a rabid dog.

Chapter 36

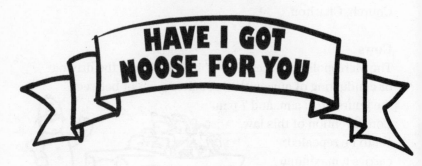

HAVE I GOT NOOSE FOR YOU

Until relocated to Newgate Prison in 1783, guilty prisoners were taken for public execution to the 'hanging tree' at Tyburn. The gallows, erected close to what is now Marble Arch, were taken down and are thought to have been used to make stands for the beer barrels in the cellar of the nearby Carpenters Arms pub. As far as pulling a pint goes, you could say it's a case of 'stands and deliver'.

And on that note, have I got noose for you...

Execution Dock

Having been sentenced to death in the Admiralty courts, from the early fifteenth century until 1830, pirates, smugglers and mutinous seamen were paraded from Marshalsea Prison in Southwark to be publicly executed at Execution Dock in Wapping. As the Admiralty's jurisdiction did not apply to dry land, the dock's hanging scaffold was erected just offshore, between Wapping New Stairs and King Henry's Stairs, on the bed of the River Thames.

Hangings were carried out with a shortened rope and,

with the drop insufficient to break the
condemned man's neck, they
would suffer a slow death, their
bodies often performing
what was known as the
'Marshal's Dance' as
their limbs shivered or
'danced' in the throes
of death. The prisoners'
bodies were then tied to
a stake and left while the
river's tide washed over their heads at least three times.

Filled with water and horribly inflated, somewhat watery
legend has it that their appearance – combined with their
location in what was a Saxon settlement known as Waeppa
– gave rise to the word 'whopper'.

In 1701, the notorious pirate Captain Kidd met his end at
Execution Dock and his body was left on display in an iron
cage for more than 20 years.

Magpie and Stump
Until public executions were abolished in 1868, the Magpie
and Stump pub at 18 Old Bailey used to serve special
'hanging breakfasts' upstairs, where diners could enjoy
unhindered views of the executions held across the street
outside Newgate Prison.

With the prison demolished in 1903 and replaced by
the famed 'Old Bailey' Central Criminal Court, the Magpie
and Stump has since become a popular haunt of lawyers;
so popular that – with the Central Criminal Court housing
courts 1 to 9 – one of the pub's rooms has unofficially
become known as Old Bailey Court No. 10.

The Magdala

On 10 April 1955, Ruth Ellis shot her lover, David Blakely, outside The Magdala pub in South Hill Park, Hampstead. Court evidence at the time stated that two of the six shots from Ellis's gun hit Blakely, while one hit a bystander and the remaining three hit the wall outside the pub. With the bullet holes still visible, on inspection one might mistakenly think that Ellis was wielding a one-inch-calibre elephant rifle: the most obvious, and yet somewhat large holes once secured a commemorative plaque, since stolen. The story of Blakely's murder was later told in the 1985 film *Dance with a Stranger*.

Following sentencing, Ellis found posthumous fame as the last woman to be hanged in the UK. Coincidentally, the second-to-last woman to be hanged in the UK, Styllou Christofi, lived barely a short rope length away from The Magdala, at 11 South Hill Park. Christofi was executed in December 1954, four months before Ellis shot Blakely, having hit her daughter-in-law over the head with an ash pan from the boiler, strangling her and – in an attempt to hide her crime – dragging the body into the back garden, before dousing it in paraffin and setting it alight.

John 'Half-Hanged' Smith

Convicted on two counts of housebreaking, in 1705 John Smith was taken to Tyburn Gallows and hanged. With the executioner not on the best of form and Smith still alive after 15 minutes, the crowd called out for his reprieve. A reprieve was duly granted and Smith was cut down and revived, gaining the nickname John 'Half-Hanged' Smith.

Granted freedom, Smith went on to be rearrested for further housebreaking but, due to complications in court, he was once again released.

Arrested for a third time and facing the gallows once more, legend tells us that on the day before his execution, the case prosecutor died and Smith was once again set free.

Eventually, after being caught stealing a padlock, John 'half-hanged-and-extremely-lucky' Smith was deported to the American state of Virginia.

Chapter 37

ON HER MAJESTY'S NOT-SO-SECRET SERVICE

Commonly known as the Brompton Oratory, the Church of the Immaculate Heart of Mary rests close to the Victoria and Albert Museum on the Brompton Road, South Kensington. According to the written accounts of a number of former Russian spies, the Oratory was widely used during the Cold War to relay secret information to Moscow. Microfilms, documents and coded messages would be left in the 'dead drop' – a small space between two pillars and the front wall of the church, close to the Pietà statue.

Time to reopen the files on some of the capital's top spy stories...

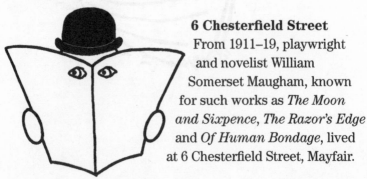

6 Chesterfield Street
From 1911–19, playwright and novelist William Somerset Maugham, known for such works as *The Moon and Sixpence*, *The Razor's Edge* and *Of Human Bondage*, lived at 6 Chesterfield Street, Mayfair.

Rather lesser known is that Maugham worked for a number of years as a British secret-service agent.

3 Audley Square

In the 1950s, while producers Cubby Broccoli and Harry Saltzman were working on the James Bond film *Dr No* in offices at 3 Audley Square in Mayfair, unbeknown to them, Russian spies were using the little trapdoor in the side of the lamp post outside the building to leave and collect secret messages.

American Gardens

Walk out the back door of the Church of the Immaculate Conception in Farm Street, Mayfair, and you'll find yourself in Mount Street Gardens, often referred to as the 'American Gardens'. Story tells that in the 1940s and 1950s, double-crossing British spy Anthony Blunt used the gardens to pass on secret documents to the Russians.

257

The Ping-Pong Ball Conspiracy

Looking for a new bus system for the country's capital, Havana, Che Guevara – at the time Cuba's finance minister – placed an order for 450 British Leyland buses. Coming at the height of the Cuban Missile Crisis, the sale and export defied a United States trade embargo and – after much tut-tutting and heavy breathing on the part of the US government – on 27 October 1964, the East German ship *Magdeburg*, with 42 buses on board, eventually set sail for Cuba from the Port of London.

From here the story is shrouded in mystery. According to certain accounts, in thick fog the *Magdeburg* soon collided with the Japanese freighter *Yamashiro Maru* and promptly sank. The buses were later recovered from the River Thames, raised to the surface – legend tells – by filling them with ping-pong balls.

Mystery still surrounds the *Magdeburg*'s sinking, with the conspiracy finger of suspicion pointing towards CIA involvement.

Section 7

AND FINALLY...

Chapter 38

LONDON LEFTOVERS

On 27 June 1967, actor Reg Varney, popularly remembered
for his role as Stan Butler in the TV sitcom *On the Buses*,
declared the world's first ATM cashpoint open. To withdraw
a maximum of ten £1 notes from the machine – outside
Barclays Bank in Church Street, Enfield – a customer would
have to insert a paper cheque impregnated with the mildly
radioactive substance carbon-14. Amid health concerns,
inventor John Shepherd-Barron calculated that a person
would have to consume 136,000 of the paper cheques before
suffering any ill effects.

On that filling note, time to delve into a few of London's
leftovers...

James Lock & Co.

First doffing its cap to passing trade in 1676 and moving to its
present site in 1764, it was from James Lock & Company in St
James's Street, Piccadilly, that Admiral Lord Nelson placed an
order for a special hat: to protect his one working eye from
the sun, the hat was to include a built-in eyeshade.

It was from the same hat makers that the Duke of Wellington bought the plumed hat that he wore in 1815 at the Battle of Waterloo.

In 1849, a man by the name of Edward Coke placed an order for a hat from Lock & Co. Coke requested that the hat be close-fitting and low-crowned in order that, while on horseback, it offered protection to his gamekeepers' heads from low-hanging branches. Lock & Co. commissioned hat makers Thomas and William Bowler to design the hat, and so was born the 'bowler', until the latter half of the twentieth century the standard headwear of the City gentleman.

Walk into James Lock & Co. and ask for a bowler and they will find it hard not to correct you as, still to this day, they refer to the hat as a 'coke', named after Edward Coke, the man that commissioned the hat.

261

Bethlem Royal Hospital

Being one of London's busiest train terminals, during the rush hour Liverpool Street station is sheer bedlam. Somewhat apt as, from 1337–1675, the station was the original site of the Bethlem Royal Hospital, more commonly known as Bedlam, one of the most infamous mental hospitals in Europe. And so it could be said that it was from the busy concourse of Liverpool Street station that the word 'bedlam' – a term to describe madness and chaos – originated.

In 1675, Bethlem Royal Hospital moved a short distance north to Moorfields. In the eighteenth century Londoners and tourists would go to Moorfields to stare at the patients and laugh at their antics. Visitors, upon payment of a one-penny entrance fee, were encouraged to poke and provoke the inmates with long sticks, and Bedlam soon became one of London's top tourist attractions.

British Library

The British Library has a collection of over eight million postage stamps, enough to cover Westminster Clock Tower. With British postage stamps carrying the head of the Queen, it could be considered appropriate that Westminster Clock Tower has been renamed the Elizabeth Tower.

Colt's Patent Firearms Manufacturing Factory

Manufacturing the gun that was said to have put the 'wild' into 'Wild West', Colonel Samuel Colt had a factory in not-so-wild Pimlico.

The factory – opened in 1853 on the site of what is now Bessborough Gardens, just north of Vauxhall Bridge – was four storeys high with a 90-metre-long sign declaring 'COLT'S PATENT FIREARMS' painted in letters over four metres in height on the roof.

Berlin Lamp

Tucked away among vegetation by the side of Westcott Lodge, to the north of Hammersmith Bridge, is a lamp post marked by a plaque. The lamp post, removed from a street in West Berlin, was given to Hammersmith in 1963 by Herr Willy Brandt before he was German Chancellor, to mark the twinning of Berlin-Neukoelin with the London suburb.

It's not recorded what Hammersmith gave in return, but do look out for missing drain covers.

The London Nobody Nose

There are, on the walls of buildings in Soho, seven sculpted noses. If you spot them all, it is said that you will attain infinite wealth.

Exactly who said this, nobody 'nose'.